# A YEAR OF

# Self-Care

## DAILY PRACTICES AND INSPIRATION FOR CARING FOR YOURSELF

Dr. Zoe Shaw

ROCKRIDGE
PRESS

For general information on our other products and services or to obtain technical support, please contact our Customer Care Department within the United States at (866) 744-2665, or outside the United States at (510) 253-0500.

Rockridge Press publishes its books in a variety of electronic and print formats. Some content that appears in print may not be available in electronic books, and vice versa.
Interior and Cover Designer: Sean Doyle
Art Producer: Sue Bischoffberger
Editor: Sean Newcott
Production Manager: Martin Worthington
Production Editor: Sigi Nacson
Illustration used under license from istockphoto.com
Author photo courtesy of Renee Bowen

ISBN: Print 978-1-64876-509-4
eBook 978-1-64739-887-3
R0

*This book is dedicated to my clients, who have given me the honor of walking with them on their personal growth and healing journey.*

# Contents

Introduction                                    ix

January: Reset                                   1

February: **Relationships**                     23

March: Renewal                                  45

April: **Motivation**                           65

May: Simplicity                                 87

June: Encouragement                            105

July: Purpose                                  125

August: Discipline                             143

September: Boundaries                          165

October: **Affirmation**                       187

November: Gratitude                            207

December: Rest                                 225

Resources                                      243

Self-care is never a selfish act—it is simply good stewardship of the only gift I have, the gift I was put on earth to offer others.

—PARKER PALMER

# *Introduction*

**Welcome to the first day of your year of self-care!**

You probably picked up this book because you have a good idea about what self-care is and feel you need more of it in your life. Or maybe you haven't been so diligent about doing what you know is good for you, and you need some accountability. *A Year of Self-Care* can offer you both.

Whether you are starting on New Year's Day or in the middle of the summer, you are giving yourself the gift of your life back.

Allow me to introduce myself. I'm Dr. Zoe, a licensed psychotherapist, mom of five, wife, advice columnist, motivational speaker, and podcast host. I help my clients find strength in challenging relationships, including that sometimes difficult relationship with themselves. The most rewarding part of my work is walking on a self-love and strength-building journey with my clients. I am often asked: *How do you do it all?* My answer is self-care. I could never do all the things that I do, take care of all the people I take care of, give what I give, and have the strong mental health that I have if I didn't care for myself first.

In this book, I will be sharing 366 motivating self-care exercises (an extra one for leap year, for good measure), supportive strategies, insightful reflections, inspirational quotes, and encouraging affirmations to help you commit to your daily self-care practice.

You can set aside 15 minutes per day—preferably in the morning to prime your mind for self-care—to read the daily entry and live it out with intent, purpose, and passion. By committing to 15 minutes, you will have devoted a little more than 91 hours of self-care over the course of the year! This investment will keep you moving on the path toward your healthiest life.

Because you need to make self-care a purposeful activity in your life, some days you will focus on prepping for a future self-care item, appointment, or activity. Even the planning is presented in such a way as to make it super simple for you to do. The daily entries will occasionally ask you to write a response to a question or prompt, so I encourage you to keep a notebook or journal on hand for deeper self-reflection. This is not just about checking off the box of self-care. It's about recharging and replenishing yourself.

Embarking on a year of self-care will allow you to fill up your emotional and mental tank and continue to top it off every day so that you're never running on low. My hope and prayer for you is that you will continue to love and invest in yourself long after you finish reading this book. I'm confident that you will, because you'll experience the rich rewards of a healthier and happier life and mindset that you deserve.

Remember that although this book is a fantastic resource to jump-start your self-care practice, it is not a replacement for a therapist, medication, or medical treatment. The daily entries are quick approaches to self-care, but any ongoing or debilitating sadness, anxiety, or depression should be addressed by a medical professional. This book can be a wonderful adjunct to therapy, but there is no shame in seeking help or treatment if you need it.

It's also important to remember that your self-care doesn't have to—and shouldn't—look like anyone else's. Feel empowered to make self-care your own.

## What Is Self-Care?

Most people think of practicing self-care when they are feeling stressed, overwhelmed, sad, or out of shape. Some people are reminded that they need to take care of themselves or know deep down that they can love themselves better.

Self-care is not as simple as a spa day. Putting on a clay mask and sipping cucumber water will not provide you with deep restorative health if you're working 50-plus hours a week and juggling a million other things.

Self-care is a daily exercise—one that is free, but priceless. It is a reckoning with your soul where you declare: *I am worthy to be cared for.*

Self-care is also not just about your physical self. Strong people take care of their body, mind, emotion, and soul. A proper self-care routine must encompass all four aspects or else it's like driving a car with only three wheels—it just won't work well to get you where you need to go.

I became dedicated to my self-care after a long, winding journey that took me down dark roads of caring for everyone but myself. At the time, I believed that I didn't have time to take care of myself and that I didn't know how to make self-care a priority. I believed that taking care of those around me—both solving their problems and making them feel cared for—was more important than my needs.

Even though I knew the basic in-flight safety rule of putting an oxygen mask on myself first, I couldn't translate that knowledge into action, because nobody had ever told me how to truly care for myself! I kept going at my standard but intense pace, depleted and burned out. I was angry and resentful, holding out hope that the people in my life would eventually take care of me.

I finally hit a breaking point; I was ready to ditch my marriage and radically rearrange my life to gain my sense of self back. Instead, that's when I developed the strength to use my words as a means of self-care. I started to speak the truth about what I was no longer willing to accept. Through the proverbial skinning of my knees, I learned how to put on my own oxygen mask first. This is what I will teach you to do in *A Year of Self-Care*, through daily directives on how to successfully self-care for an entire year. By the end of this book, you will have developed the habit of investing in yourself every single day and become a self-care master.

It's important to note that embracing self-care doesn't mean you have to nearly lose everything important to you in order to achieve a life you love. Wisdom is gained in one of two ways: learning from your own mistakes or from the mistakes of others. I'm going to help you gain the wisdom of self-care the easy, healthy way. Self-care is not just a designated time of the day when you focus on yourself—it's a habit of valuing yourself in all of your interactions and being productive throughout your day. Through these core self-care methods, you can earn greater respect from the people in your life, decrease instances of illness; increase self-confidence, strength, and resiliency; and achieve a greater sense of calm. I trust that you will come to love that your relationship with yourself and others is centered around and in alignment with your priorities and values.

There is no greater gift to give yourself than a calm, centered mind and a strong, limber body full of energy to accomplish all that you want. By focusing on your well-being, you will improve your health, increase your happiness, foster spirituality, establish healthy boundaries and relationships, define and embrace your values, and prioritize your own self-growth.

And you will give those gifts to yourself through your self-care. It's an honor to walk with you for an entire year on a path to self-care. I am already so excited for you to experience the life transformation that comes from making your self-care a priority.

## Before You Get Started

Repeat the following self-care pact aloud, today or any day that you are embarking on self-care, and embrace the journey ahead:

*I will not simply check off the self-care box. I am far more valuable and complicated than an item to be checked off. I commit to the deep, caring experience of getting to know myself intimately. I will enjoy the ride. Today, I solemnly swear that I will practice self-care in a meaningful way.*

# Reset

**Reset, readjust, restart, refocus as many times as you need to.**

—UNKNOWN

Happy New You! The first month of the year is about resetting and creating new self-care habits that will lay the foundation for all of your self-care practices throughout the year.

I gently but strongly discourage you from making the traditional New Year's resolutions that are attached to a number on the scale, dress size, credit score, relationship status, or bank balance. Instead, use this month to focus on the journey of healthy living and how that will positively affect your true resolutions. It's not really about seeing results that can be quantified; it's about feeling the results in your soul. The ripple effect of self-care will eventually show itself in measurable ways as well, but without the guilt or pressure of deadlines.

This is your year. Your year for growth. Your year to release the old and bring forth your potential.

Take five minutes to journal what you expect to be qualitatively differ-ent about yourself one year from now. What will you discover? What will you accomplish? How will you best take care of yourself?

When the year starts, your mind is often motivated for a new beginning and all the possible gifts this year has. This January, let your desire for newness help you move forward as you get your physical body into a healthy alignment with your mind.

The theme for your self-care this month will be resetting. You deserve to feel excited about this, because the best change is created in incremental steps. Each step may seem small, but every day you'll be building a strong base of self-care that will give you all the strength you need to create the life you want.

In the words of Arthur Ashe, "Start where you are. Use what you have. Do what you can."

# 1

## Goals, Goals, Goals

Goals, aspirational but still concrete, are different from resolutions. Today, you know what you want, and you're willing to go on a self-care journey to get there. Let's get started by identifying a clear, purpose-driven reason for your goals; then write them down, which will make it more likely that you will manifest them. Why do you want to self-care? What do you intend to get out of this year? Do you want to feel more rested, more centered, more cared for and loved? Do you want to move in a healthier body, get more sleep?

Find motivation in this well-known quote: "When you feel like quitting, think about why you started."

# 2

## I am . . .

This is a grounding exercise that centers you to the present. Take off your shoes and sit on a chair, couch, or bench. Press your bare feet into the floor or ground beneath you. Raise both of your hands above your head. Gently lower them straight down, pressing them firmly into the surface on which you are sitting. Now speak the following affirmation:

*I am a vessel of strength, joy, and resiliency. I fill up myself daily so that I can serve myself and my people in the way in which I was created. Like a cocooned butterfly, I am growing and changing in the most beautiful ways.*

Repeat this affirmation during your day.

# 3

## Your Appointment

Self-care is about planning to make yourself a priority.

Today, as a means of self-care, schedule a checkup with your doctor. If you've already had a visit within the last six months, make your next appointment.

Ask about getting your routine blood work done, including panels to check your vitamin levels to detect deficiencies that could require supplementation or nutritional adjustments. Remember, your body is the vessel in which you live your life. Maintaining it is the key to having the life you want.

After you've made the appointment, take a moment to feel proud of taking care of yourself.

# 4

## A New Perspective

It's so easy to get stuck in a rut or to zone out on autopilot. Today, give yourself the gift of a new perspective.

Take a different route to work, another way to school, or an alternate path for a jog. Express gratitude as you take in the new scenes, staying active, engaged, and aware in your life. What do you see? Can you stop and smell the roses?

# 5

## Media-less Morning

The first hour of your morning sets the foundation for the rest of the day. Set the stage clean, focused, and clear of distractions and bombardments on your psyche. Today, for one hour after you awake, resist the urge to reach for your phone. Reach instead for a book or journal.

Consider making a pact every morning not to touch your devices until after you've begun your day with a centering routine, such as meditation, writing, or exercise.

# 6

~

## Hydration

Decide how much water you want to consume during the day to stay properly hydrated and healthy.

A good trick to meet your goal: Fill up your water bottle every morning and focus on finishing it before you have breakfast. Then, fill it up again, and sip on it slowly throughout the day. This will keep you motivated to get in your water intake early.

Drink up!

# 7

~

**Every day, each of us is faced with the possibility of resetting our lives. Refocusing. Reimagining. Rebooting. Every day, we can decide to change our outlook, our words, our tone, and our attitude.**

—MARIA SHRIVER

# 8

~

## Embrace Sleep

I encourage you to think about what sleep means to you. Is it a precious gift? A scary unknown? A forced time-out? A frustrating struggle? Let's improve your relationship with sleep.

Today, do one thing that makes your room a more inviting place of comfort. You could set up an oil diffuser, put a few drops of essential lavender oil on your pillow, declutter a bedroom area, remove the presence of lights from electronics, start a 15-minute routine that calms you before bedtime, or use a sleep tracker to gain an understanding of your sleep patterns.

An improved relationship with sleep means a better relationship with yourself.

JANUARY

# 9

~

## Reconnect

Take a moment today to put away your devices and distractions, go outside, look up at the sky, and breathe. You'll find that just gazing upward at the open sky for a few minutes allows you to disconnect from noise and obligations. Take in the sun and the clouds, or even the dark night sky speckled with stars, to ground your soul and feel connected with something greater than yourself.

JANUARY

# 10

~

## You Are a Visionary

Start a vision board today. No need to cut up magazines—you can create one online easily. Visualization is a potent tool for designing the life you want The purpose of your vision board is to bring all of the aspirational and inspiring images to fruition in your actual life.

Focus the content of your vision board on how you want to feel in addition to what you want to manifest in your life. Create it in a way that is self-caring, motivational, and loving.

*I am powerful. I have the power to create all the change that I want. I have the wisdom to determine what I need to let go of and what I need to keep and honor.*

## Be Grateful

Place a clear jar on your nightstand or desk. Every day, on a small piece of paper, write down one thing you are grateful for (just a word or two) or a word of encouragement, fold up the paper, and put it in the jar. Halfway through the year, return to your gratitude jar and read the many things you were grateful for, remembering that your self-care practice is a journey with no judgment.

# 13

## Stretch

Stretching is not just for athletes: It's crucial for maintaining a body that moves through the world with ease. Stretching decreases joint pain and increases range of motion. Without a regular stretching practice, your muscles shorten and are more prone to injury.

Take a break to stretch for 15 minutes. Play some calming music and extend your limbs in any way that feels good. Push yourself until you feel some resistance, but not pain. Hold and breathe.

# 14

## Create Your Cave

Create a self-care nook in your home—a special and quiet space that you can make your own. It could be a corner in a closet, a favorite chair in the living room, or a cleared-out area in the attic. In this place, you can meditate, journal, and create meaningful art, whatever feels best and most comforting. However—and wherever—you choose to set up your spot, make it yours.

# 15

## You Are the Author

Become the writer of your own story. You are the author of your life. As you go about your day, think of all the wonderful and empowering ways that you influence your narrative. If you have incorporated journaling into self-care, take time to write down some of the ways you controlled your story today.

# 16

## A Playlist for Your Heart

Music expresses the longing of your soul. There is something very transformative about the way musical rhythm connects to the beating of your own heart. Care for yourself today by creating a playlist of songs that touches that deep place in you, creates harmony, or makes you feel happy or calm. Listen deeply without any distractions. And feel free to add to it regularly as you discover new music that speaks to you.

## 17

# Take a Walk

Walking is the simplest and most natural form of exercise. Go on a nice, long walk today, to or from your usual destinations. Focus on feeling thankful for the way your body moves and its ability to take you where you need to go.

## 18

# Reset

Treat yourself with grace and kindness, recognizing that this month of reset-ting is a journey. Start fresh every day. Yesterday no longer exists except in your memory. It may not have been that great, but judging yourself about your choices is a waste of your precious time and energy.

As you swing your legs out of bed every morning, say,

*Thank you for the gift of a new day. Tomorrow is behind me. I look forward to opening the gift of today.*

# 19

## Do One Thing

Perhaps you envision power in multitasking. Resist the urge to juggle too many tasks today. Care for yourself by doing one thing at a time. Focus on being present as you attend to all things today. Evaluate whether this works better for you—for your sense of accomplishment, your feeling of pride, or your level of energy at the end of the day.

# 20

## You Are Perfection

Do you shy away from your true self? Consider caring for yourself today by being more of you. What does that mean? Pay attention to all of the ways that you censor yourself, the times you don't speak up, or the moments you believe that you are "too much." You are perfect as you are.

Today is a day to become more of who you were created to be. Today, be more of you.

# 21

## Do the Hard Thing

Do something hard today. Confront an issue, speak up for the underdog, voice the truth when a lie is easier. Strength comes from making difficult choices or navigating unknown paths. You are caring for yourself when you choose strength-building actions that promote growth. Watch yourself grow.

# 22

## Heal

The most powerful way to heal is to make changes to your lifestyle. Consider how you are caring for yourself today with the foods you put in your mouth, the way you move your body, and the thoughts you choose to allow into your consciousness.

# 23

~

Every sunset is an opportunity to reset. Every sunrise begins with new eyes.

—RICHIE NORTON

# 24

~

*I am brave, courageous, and dare to be different. I am a magnet that is easily and effortlessly drawn toward all that I need to create the life I dream of. I am proud of who I am becoming.*

## 25

# News Fast

Take an entire day off from the news. Avoid it on all of your devices. Consider that you won't miss a thing, except for some negativity. Pay attention to how it feels not to take in news of conflict, violence, or corruption. If it seems like a positive act of self-care, consider making a regular habit of fasting from the news.

## 26

# You Are Enough

You may think you have to look outside of yourself for the answers. However, you have all that you need: a conscious, logical mind and a caring heart. You are enough.

# 27

## Go Somewhere in Your Mind

Books are a great source of self-care and can take you to new, inspiring places. With a good book, you can travel across the world, time, and space. A great read can also teach you a skill, entertain you, or challenge your soul.

Where do you want to be transported to next? Make a list of books that can take you there, and commit to a reading schedule. If you start a book and you don't love the journey it's taking you on, put it down and pick up the next one. When you finish a book, donate it and acquire a new one.

# 28

**If you want to have a life that is worth living, a life that expresses your deepest feelings and emotions and cares and dreams, you have to fight for it.**

—ALICE WALKER

# 29

## This Is Yours

Self-care doesn't happen to you, nor is it something you fall into. It is not a gift that anyone can give you. It's an intentional choice you make every day to honor the creation of your being and give yourself what you need so that you can be what you were made to be in this world. Self-care is not selfish, but you do have to fight for it. Fight in the most beautiful, calm, quiet, internal way.

JANUARY

# 30

~

## It's All Good

When asked who your greatest influence is, you may be tempted to name a family member, a dear friend, a teacher, or a current or former romantic partner. But no matter how formative these people may have been in your life, your greatest influence is you.

The self-talk you practice reaches as far back as your childhood and extends to this exact moment. The more positive your self-talk is, the healthier your life is. Positive self-talk is one of the best forms of self-care. Pay attention today to how you speak to yourself and the stories you tell yourself about what's happening in your life. If it ever feels like being negative is easier than being positive, flip the script. Find the positive. It's like you're giving yourself a mental massage.

# 31

## You're Special

Do you have a favorite accessory or item of clothing that you save for a special occasion? Wear it today. You are a special occasion. You deserve it. You are moving forward on your self-care journey. You are growing into what you were created to be!

# Relationships

**Have enough courage to trust love one more time and always one more time.**

—MAYA ANGELOU

This month is about loving yourself and investing in your relationships in a healthy way. If that sounds too indulgent, remember that when you love yourself, you have the fullness to approach your relationships from a place of calm and well-being rather than desperation and codependency.

Throughout your life, you may have received messages that programmed you to dislike yourself or told you that your needs were a burden. This month is about recasting those messages into a unified voice that shouts, *My needs are a beautiful, necessary expression of my humanity; they are important, and I will never silence them again.*

True strength and confidence are actually quiet—they don't need to scream to be heard—but sometimes you need to shout, internally or otherwise, to start believing in something healthier.

This month is your declaration to love yourself and others well.

# 1

## You're the One You've Been Looking For

Make a list of all the things you love about yourself. If you're struggling to start, try this reason as number one: *I love that I care about myself enough to seek the help I need to stay healthy.*

It's okay if loving yourself feels challenging at first. Every self-care act, big or small, will prove to you that you are worthy of loving. Remember, your mind believes what you tell it.

## 2

# You Are Worthy

You are worthy of healthy life-giving relationships. Speaking positive thoughts, even when you don't believe them, has a powerful effect on your life.

Thinking of people in a positive way—even just for a day—affects your experience with them. Today, act as if you adore everyone with whom you come into contact. This is not about pretending or being inauthentic. This is an act of positively influencing your mind. Observe the difference this makes in how you respond to others and how they respond to you.

## 3

# Date Yourself

You are an interesting, multidimensional person, and you should enjoy your own company. Take yourself on a date: Go to a restaurant, a museum, a café, or a park—somewhere you can spend time and get to know yourself a little bit better. Embrace the reflective silence of your own company, or bring a thought-provoking book, music, or craft with you to enjoy.

FEBRUARY

# 4

## The V-Word

Vulnerability can be scary, but it is also a liberating means of self-care. If you avoid vulnerability, you effect more damage than you realize by keeping yourself closed off to new opportunities, people, and ideas. Take a chance and have the courage to experiment with vulnerability.

Being vulnerable is easier than you think. When you dance with abandon, you are being vulnerable and declaring that you accept yourself. When you say what you truly feel, you are making a statement that your emotions and entire being matter. Reflect on what vulnerability means to you, and embrace thinking of vulnerability as a means of honoring yourself. Think of ways that you can support others in expressing their own vulnerability.

FEBRUARY

# 5

~

## Pick Up the Phone

Perhaps you haven't spoken to a friend in a while. You've caught yourself thinking of them every now and then, and you know you should call, but you haven't gotten around to it. Cultivate that friendship today; pick up the phone and call them to say hello and check in on them. Instead of putting off the call for another day, or absentmindedly texting them, invest in the effort to phone them now. Honor the importance of your relationships.

FEBRUARY

# 6

~

## These Are for You

Buy yourself a bouquet of flowers—whatever catches your eye, smells best, or brings you joy. Every time you see them, even if your home feels cluttered or it's a chaotic day, they will give you a sense of calm and comfort.

# 7

## Say It Out Loud

Tell the people you love that you love them. Your verbal expression of devotion is the glue that holds relationships together. It will not only lift their spirits to hear that they are loved, but it will also fill your own heart with gratitude that you have such meaningful people in your life.

FEBRUARY

# 8

## The most important relationship is the one you have with yourself.

—DIANE VON FURSTENBERG

# 9

## Move with a Friend

Exercise should be a loving gift to your body. Rather than focusing on a specific goal or feeling like you're at war with yourself, choose exercise as a way to love and honor your body. Ask a friend to exercise with you—whether it's a walk, a run, or an exercise class—and enjoy cultivating relationships around movement. Life is good when you move with a friend.

# 10

## Tune In

Paying attention to your body, understanding your natural rhythms, learning to inhale and exhale at the right time—this is called deep listening. To ignore the body's signals denies you access to a part of yourself. You wouldn't have a healthy relationship with a friend who always ignored you, and the same goes for your relationships with yourself. Get into a habit of asking your body what it needs to better honor your relationship with yourself.

## Face the World

Today, imagine yourself standing on the top of a mountain and looking fiercely at the world and saying, *I am here for a purpose. I matter. I am worth it. I am taking care of this body and soul.*

## Self-love is embracing the broken parts of you, instead of trying to fix them.

—LESLIE DWIGHT

## Love Letter

There's nothing that makes you feel more adored and cared for than a love letter sent to you by your favorite person.

Write a love letter to yourself. Think about the amazing, quirky, unique, and beautiful things about you, and write them all down. Detail the ways you love and appreciate yourself. When you finish the letter, address it, add a stamp, and mail it to yourself. You deserve it!

## Sleep Mantra

Go to bed 30 minutes earlier than you normally would tonight. Put on cozy pajamas, turn out the lights, and make sure your bed is as comfortable as it can be. As you lie in your bed, repeat the following until you fall asleep: *I love who I am. I accept who I am. I am thankful for who I am.* When you wake up in the morning, pay attention to how much lighter and more well rested you feel.

FEBRUARY

# 15

*I am worthy of love because I exist. Others reflect and respond to the love that I have for myself.*

FEBRUARY

# 16

## Move Quickly

Move your body quickly for 10 minutes—do a dance, sprint for a few minutes, whatever feels best. Exercising for quick, intense bursts can be more effective than long sessions of lower-intensity movement. Exercise also increases the production of serotonin, one of the main components in most antidepressants. Move quickly to treat yourself to feeling good.

# 17

## Be Complimentary

Give yourself a compliment today. Did your hair turn out great this morning? Does that dress accentuate your beautiful curves? Are you impressed with how you handled your disgruntled client? Speak it out loud. Tell yourself, *Good job! I'm proud of you.*

# 18

## Loving Massage

Try your own Ayurveda self-massage *abhyanga* at home. *Abhyanga* is lovingly anointing yourself from head to toe with warm oil, which can create a feeling of stability and warmth.

Warm some oil, adding your favorite essential oil. Sit or stand comfortably on the floor in a warm room or in your bathtub. Apply the oil to the top of your head, massaging it into your scalp. Next, massage your entire face with oil, including your lips and ears. Use long, circular strokes over your entire body from your neck down. Finish with your feet and toes. Lie quietly for about 15 minutes, allowing the warm oil to soak into your skin and body. Take a relaxing shower to remove excess oil, then gently pat down your body.

# 19

## Release Your Ego

Consider the most important relationship that you have. Today, as you interact with that person, release your need to be right. Focus deeply on what that person is saying. Take an interest in what interests them. Check in with yourself and see if this fills you up. It truly is better to give than to receive—especially in cherished relationships.

# 20

## You Can Never Have Too Many Friends

We're built for connection. The proven benefits of social connection include lower rates of anxiety and depression, heightened self-esteem, stronger immune systems, and increased longevity and quality of life. Although forming new friendships in adulthood takes a little more intention, the payoff is worth it. There are even apps for finding new platonic friendships in your area. Be open to new relationships today and look for opportunities to connect with people.

# 21

## Take a Tea Break

Make a warm cup of tea. Take a moment to inhale the fragrant steam before you take a sip. Pair it with a good book, some soft music, and a comfy chair. This is you exhaling. Clear your mind of any to-dos—they'll still be there when you are finished enjoying a moment to yourself. Focus on calming, caring thoughts. You are worthy of all the attention you give yourself. Caring for yourself is saying, *I love me.*

## 22

~

# Intentional Eating

Eat with intention today. Eating is a sacred act that is often rushed without much care. When you take in food, you are loving and caring for your body. Today, eat in a calm, comforting, quiet environment. Do not multitask or distract yourself with devices. Set aside time to truly receive your meal. Savor the flavor. Roll each bite around on your tongue slowly before swallowing. Visualize your digestive system taking in the food and assimilating it within your body. Imagine all of the nutrients filling up the necessary spaces. Notice the signals your body sends when it is satisfied, then stop eating. When you are finished, take deep breaths and give thanks for your sustenance.

# 23

## Just Say It

Talk about the hard things today. You don't grow from a place of comfort. Care for yourself by being willing to speak the things often unspoken. It may not feel great in the moment, but you are creating long-term freedom, intimacy, health, and wellness for you and your relationships by releasing what needs to be spoken.

# 24

## Nurture Your Heart Space

Practice rubbing your heart space for five minutes. Slowly rub over your heart in large circular motions, applying as much pressure as feels comfortable. Close your eyes and breathe deeply in and out.

Think about how your heart organ supports your existence. Your heart organ is closely connected with your brain. In fact, your heart sends more messages to your brain (neurologically) than your brain sends to your heart, making it unlike any other organ in your body. Your heart responds immediately to your emotional state, speeding up, slowing down, skipping a beat. Perhaps that is why the psychological foundation of love is referred to as "heart." Love on your heart today.

# 25

## Cuddle Up

Hold and cuddle yourself for a few minutes. Find the coziest blanket and the most comfortable space, and feel warm, held, and comforted. This is you loving yourself.

# 26

## The Personal Wish List

Write a personal message—or mantra—that expresses gratitude for your health and opportunities. Include a wish for well-being, prosperity, and peace for yourself and for those whom you love most. End with your greatest desire. Memorize this message and repeat it to yourself when you need to feel grounded.

# 27

## Do New

Plan to do something new with your loved ones that you've never done before. It could be volunteering for a cause, trying a different restaurant, or taking a day trip to a never-before-seen place. Feel free to get creative and enjoy where the adventure takes you.

# 28

*I am good enough. I love myself. The ways that I choose to care for myself are good enough.*

# 29

## Sing Your Own Song

As you close this month of focusing on relationships, remember that the relationship you have with yourself is the foundation for all of your other relationships. You are the one most capable of learning the song of your heart and singing it to yourself when you become a little lost.

Do you know what your love language is? Is it affirmations, acts of service, receiving gifts, quality time, or physical touch? You can give all of these to yourself and will love others more brilliantly in the process. Love yourself well. Now and always.

# Renewal

**Renewal requires opening yourself up to new ways of thinking and feeling.**

—DEBORAH DAY

March marks the end of winter and the beginning of spring, a time when all of life's potential, buried underground, pushes its way to the surface and the world seems to be born anew. There is a sense of hope in this season that propels you forward.

Make March a month of renewal. It's the perfect time to focus on taking the best, loving care of your mental health. Meditate on mental health as your state of well-being. Operating from a state of well-being assists you in realizing your true potential. You are better equipped to cope with life's stressors and successfully work toward giving back to yourself, your loved ones, and your community.

Because there's an intimate connection between your mind and body, this month focus on improving your mental health, which will in turn enhance your overall health.

Focus on these universally known words of wisdom: "The only way to change it is to do something different." You've got this!

# 1

*I am refreshed and energized to live my life in a purposeful, new, healthy way.*

# 2

## Talk to Yourself

You likely have a passive voice in your head—a collection of all the voices you have heard over your lifetime that plays in a constant loop. Today, instead of passively listening to any negative self-talk, take control and talk to yourself. Push back against your inner critic with positive truths, such as, *I am full of life—refreshed, rejuvenated, and reborn—and I am doing a great job today.*

## 3

## Coloring to Feel Calm

When was the last time you colored in a coloring book? It's not just for kids! Coloring calms anxiety and increases focus. Explore the multitude of relaxing coloring books for adults. Find a favorite, grab a variety of colored pencils, and feel the calm wash over you.

## 4

**We delight in the beauty of a butterfly but rarely admit the changes it has gone through to achieve that beauty.**

—MAYA ANGELOU

# 5

## Get Some Z's

Care for yourself by taking a well-deserved nap. There are few activities that hold the rejuvenating power of a quick nap. A midday nap can restore alertness, enhance your performance, and even reduce your chance of a heart attack. Power napping for 20 to 30 minutes is the ideal way to bolster energy and harness the benefits of a midday rest without interfering with your sleep routine (circadian rhythms). Try fitting one in today.

# 6

## Sing It Out!

As you shower, play your all-time favorite song, and sing along loudly. Enjoy connecting with the music and gifting yourself with a little concert as you begin your day. Lather, rinse, and repeat. Life is good.

# Watch and Learn

Everyone has a "thing" that defines their life experience. Each person's thing is unique. Some are apparent and others are invisible. It may be an addiction, a health issue, a special needs child, a difficult marriage, childhood trauma, a conflicting value, or a mental health issue.

Your responsibility is to care for yourself and to feel compassion for the struggles of others, even if you're unaware of what those struggles are. Learn all you can about your unique issue. Become the expert on how to care for yourself, and don't hesitate to reach out to professionals for help if you need it.

MARCH

8

# Laugh It Out

When you are feeling sad, make yourself laugh. It may feel silly at first, but laughter is powerful medicine. Once you begin laughing, your mood will brighten.

This little trick works even if you aren't feeling bad. Let yourself laugh for one minute and see how much it can improve your day.

# 9

## What Do You Sense?

Take a few minutes to focus on all five of your senses and ground yourself in the present moment. Ask yourself:

*What do I hear? How does that make me feel?*
*What do I see? How does that make me feel?*
*What do I touch? How does that feel?*
*What do I smell? What does that remind me of?*
*What do I taste? How does that make me feel?*

Asking yourself these questions sends a message to your brain that you care.

# 10

## Let Yourself Glow

Indulge in a warm bath with this homemade sugar scrub that will relax you and give you a glow.

### Sugar Scrub     MAKES 1 JAR

---

1 cup brown, cane, or
   raw sugar
2 or 3 tablespoons olive,
   jojoba, or almond oil
Essential oil of your choice
   (optional)
Lemon juice (optional)

1. Select the sugar of your choice (brown is the least coarse, cane is in the middle, and raw is the most abrasive), and put it in a medium bowl. Add the oil a tablespoon at a time, mixing after each addition with a fork. The ideal consistency is sand-like, not runny.

2. If desired, add a few drops of essential oil and lemon juice to the bowl. Mix well.

3. Transfer the scrub to a jar with a lid and use within a month.

# 11

## Name Your Feelings

Spend the day paying attention to your emotions by naming them. Notice how you are feeling, and name it out loud (if you can). Are you feeling calm? Frustrated?

It's important to remember that all emotions are good. Emotions give you information. If anger tells you that something is unjust, ask yourself, *What's unjust?* If sadness tells you that you have lost something, ask yourself, *What have I lost?* If anxiety tells you that you are in danger, ask yourself, *What feels threatening?*

Naming your emotions can reduce the negative effect of them. Naming them is honoring your feelings, but your feelings are not you and, once named, they are free to move on.

## MARCH

# 12

~~

**Change the way you look at things, and the things you look at change.**

—WAYNE DYER

## MARCH

# 13

~~

# Become Childlike

Do something today that you loved to do when you were a child. Finger paint, hang from the monkey bars, do a cartwheel, or jump on the bed. Tap into that carefree feeling, allowing that youthful smile to light up your face.

# 14

## Ask for Help

Sometimes you may feel convinced that if you want something done, you can rely on only yourself to do it. You may reinforce this belief by taking on too much. Asking for help can feel like a sign of weakness. It's difficult to accept assistance because you may be tempted to judge the help that you receive. Yes, you could have completed the task better, faster, and with more precision, but focus on the benefit of getting the help, not the potential of it being done imperfectly. Care for yourself by asking for help today and accepting it exactly as it comes. As Sheryl Sandberg says, "Done is better than perfect."

MARCH

# 15

*I am a deep listener to what my body needs, and I act in a loving way.*

# 16

## You Are a Good Investment

You can replace a home, a car, and other large investments, but you cannot replace your body. Investing in yourself is not a frivolous expense. It is necessary to maintain your most crucial asset. You get one body, one mind, and one soul. How can you take good care of them today?

# 17

## Guard Yourself

Although it may not always feel like it, you have the power to choose what you allow in your mind. Practice guarding your psyche today. Pay attention to the songs you listen to, the articles you read, the TV you watch, even the conversations you engage in. You are constantly taking in outside influences. You are the uncompromising gatekeeper against anything that doesn't serve your mission of self-care.

# 18

## Unload the Guilt

Guilt is like carrying around a heavy, unwanted, smelly weight. Unload that guilt today, and embrace feeling lighter. Think about something that you've been feeling guilty about—no matter how big or small. Remind yourself that guilt is about the past, which is set in stone.

You can use your knowledge gained to affect the future, which is malleable. Guilt is a wasted emotion.

You are not required to be the same person you were five minutes ago, so stand up and shake your body from head to toe. Imagine the weight of all of your guilt falling from your shoulders and creating space for more forgiving and loving thoughts.

MARCH

# 19

~

## Journal Easy

One of the best therapies for your mental health is regular journaling. Sometimes it can feel overwhelming to sit down and craft words. You may feel at a loss for what to write or how to write it. It can be tempting to censor yourself because you imagine your journal has an outside audience.

Practice journaling by writing a few words on a sticky note every day. Whatever comes to mind that day, write it down. You can start with a feeling—*I feel . . .*—and write why. It can be that easy!

MARCH

# 20

~

## Repeat, Repeat

Craft a mantra that speaks to your soul—it can be any meaningful word, phrase, or sound. Allow it to challenge that sometimes negative voice that imparts its defeating words. Sit quietly and repeat your declaration to yourself for five minutes today. Feel a sense of determined calm inhabit your being.

MARCH

# 21

## Declutter

Take 15 minutes to declutter an area of your most used space. Clutter isn't just inconvenient; it actually causes emotional drag and stress on your body, too. When you declutter your space, you declutter your mind.

MARCH

# 22

## Immerse in a Bit of Green

Consider starting a garden in your backyard, planting potted herbs on your windowsill, or joining a local community garden—however you can relate best to a green space. Be sure to let your hands get dirty. You'll be amazed at how calming and healing it is to connect with the earth.

# 23

## Change Up the Scent

Smells greatly affect your mood. Whether you are using a diffuser, essential oils, or perfumes, you may have become nose blind to a particular scent if you have used it for a long period of time.

Consider changing your scent and see how it affects your mood for the better. Here are some common scents and their effects on your system:

**Lavender** promotes relaxation and restful sleep, reduces heart rate, and soothes muscle pain.

**Bergamot** lowers cortisol (a stress hormone) and decreases depression.

**Vanilla** reduces restlessness and promotes stress relief and relaxation.

**Orange** gives you a dose of energy, reduces anxiety, and has been shown to help with PTSD symptoms.

**Lemon** reduces stress and tension and eases depression and anxiety.

## 24

# Make a Move

Ask your body what type of movement it needs today, then spend 15 minutes doing it. Dance to some music, take a walk, practice active stretching, or partake in yoga.

## 25

# Give Anonymously

Pay for the next customer's coffee without announcing it or cut your neighbor's grass while they're away. There are several ways to give. Remember that it's not the recognition that makes it worthwhile, but the act of giving itself.

# 26

## What Is Enough?

Do you live in a continual state of trying—seeking, waiting, hoping, and wanting? Today, spend some time journaling, asking yourself, What is enough? Tune out your wildest hopes and dreams for a minute. Instead, focus on what is enough. You gain a sense of well-being from feeling full in life. Is it possible that you already have it?

# 27

## Break Away

If you are constantly distracting yourself, it means you need to heal from something. Take a break from all screens for three full days. It takes this long for the effects of changed patterns to reset your system.

This break from technology may create some scary, empty space. Your mind will want you to reach for your phone for diversion. Don't. Sit with the feeling instead. There is a reason why you distract yourself. It's time for you to identify, honor, and work through your feelings to heal.

## You Choose

Acknowledge the power of the role that you play in your own life. There will forever be happenings that you can't control, but you always have choices that determine how you experience life. You ultimately choose your life, not by the external circumstances, but by determining your response.

When something bad happens, you can choose to find the good in it—a mental act called reframing. Today, work on reframing negative circumstances into positive ones. Tell yourself, *I am in control of my life. I choose the lens through which I experience the world. I can always change a lens that isn't working for me.*

## Laughter is an instant vacation.

—MILTON BERLE

MARCH

# 30

~

## **Write It Out**

Write a letter to someone who has hurt you and tell them honestly and openly how you feel. When you finish the letter, rip it up or burn it. Knowing that you won't actually send it will allow you to express your feelings without hesitation and work through them exactly as you feel them. Go ahead, get it all out. You don't need to hold that negativity anymore.

MARCH

# 31

~

*I am mentally healthy, strong, and resilient. I listen to what I need, and I lovingly give it to myself. I am a full vessel, which allows me to give freely.*

# Motivation

## You are the leader you've been looking for.

—MARIA SHRIVER

Learning how to motivate yourself is the true vehicle to accomplishing your purpose on this earth. Often, you may think you need a coach or a force outside of yourself to create true, actionable motivation, but that couldn't be further from the truth.

My dear friend, you speak to yourself more than anyone else speaks to you. And you speak to yourself more than you speak to anyone else. Therefore, you are your biggest influence for better or worse. The good news is that you know yourself best and can be an amazing cheerleader as a result. So, for the month of April, get motivated!

# 1

## Set It Up

Write down three or four goals that you want to accomplish this month. They may be part of a larger goal or goals that you wish to pursue. Remember, there is power in your spoken words. Write down your goals and post them where you'll see them often. When you do, give them a minute of focused attention. Read them out loud. Remind yourself what you are working toward achieving.

# 2

**Live with intention. Walk to the edge. Listen hard. Practice wellness. Play with abandon. Laugh. Choose with no regret. Appreciate your friends. Continue to learn. Do what you love. Live as if this is all there is.**

—MARY ANNE RADMACHER

## 3

# Visualize Your Goals

Leave your work or obligations a few minutes early. Stop by an open, green space. Sit by yourself and daydream for a few minutes about reaching your goals. Tell yourself, *I have everything I need to accomplish my goals. What I don't know, I will find out. I am manifesting my greatest desires and am grateful for the ability to do so.*

## 4

# Reverse To-do List

Instead of creating a to-do list for the day ahead, move ahead with your day and create an "I did" list when the day is done. Proudly write down all of the tasks you accomplished today, whether they were planned or spontaneous. Observe how thrilling it feels to immediately put a check mark next to every task knowing that you accomplished that much today. You are amazing!

## Get More Sleep

Sleep deprivation leaves you feeling less motivated to do all that needs to be done on any given day. You may not notice its detrimental effects, but they add up over time, wreaking havoc on your hormonal system, mental clarity, and cardiovascular health. Utilize a sleep tracker to better understand the quality of your sleep. Create a plan to get a solid seven to nine hours of sleep every night. You deserve it.

**Be miserable. Or motivate yourself. Whatever has to be done, it's always your choice.**

—WAYNE DYER

# Invigorating Cold

A cold shower might not sound like self-care at first, but it is! Cold showers awaken all your senses, which benefits your mind and body. The banya, an old Russian tradition, involves alternating between hot steam and ice-cold water. The jolt to your system is said to increase your immune response, reducing sickness in your body.

Hop in a cold shower today. While the chilliness is activating your nervous system, tell yourself, *I am alive and present and ready to* face this day!

Follow up with a comforting warm lotion and harness the energy to tackle what lies ahead.

# 8

## Reward Yourself

Setting up a reward system for accomplishing your goals feels motivational if your reward isn't counterproductive. If you've met your weight goal, don't reward yourself with cake. Buying that cute pair of jeans in your new size, how-ever, may be just what you need to keep progressing. Behavioral conditioning research has proven that rewarding successive approximations (small steps toward a bigger goal) is the best way to reinforce a behavior and create more of it. So, reward the small steps and keep on stepping.

# 9

**The jump is so frightening between where I am and where I want to be . . . because of all I may become, I will close my eyes and leap!**

—MARY ANNE RADMACHER

APRIL

# 10

## Power Nap with a Boost

It may sound counterintuitive, but experiment with drinking a little caffeine immediately prior to taking a 20-minute nap. By the time you wake up, the caffeine will have kicked in, making you feel energized and motivated, but still refreshed from your nap.

APRIL

# 11

## Eat Your Vegetables First

Make your life easy by doing the hard things first.

Tackle self-care first thing in the morning, rather than saving it for the last part of your day, when you are already tired. When you devalue yourself, relegating your needs to last on the list, resentment and burnout are not far down the road. Whether it's eating your daily intake of vegetables, filling out a spreadsheet, getting in your exercise, or setting aside some quiet time for yourself, tackle it all head-on.

APRIL

# 12

Take criticism seriously, but not personally. If there is truth or merit in the criticism, try to learn from it. Otherwise, let it roll right off you.

—HILLARY CLINTON

APRIL

# 13

## Push Yourself a Little

Use the well-known quote "Nothing worthwhile is ever easy" to motivate yourself to choose difficult tasks.

A good coach knows the balance between pushing your limits and encouraging rest. A good coach challenges you enough that you approach your limit without overdoing it. Their vision sees beyond today, and they understand well the necessity of long-term commitment to achieve success.

Be a good coach today by pushing yourself a little more than usual, while still honoring your limits.

# 14

~

## When You Give, You Get

When you motivate others, you also inspire your soul. Find someone who looks like they need some encouragement, then speak to them today. Recognize that your words are just as much for you as they are for them.

# 15

~

**In helping others, we help ourselves, for whatever good we give out completes the circle and comes back to us.**

—FLORA EDWARDS

APRIL

# 16

Find Life Inspiration

Think about a public leader, thinker, or influencer who is deeply inspiring to you. Find a biography that covers their life story, then read it. Let their story—their struggles and success—inspire you.

Think about your challenges and deficits, then consider how you can use those dark times to help others who are a few steps behind you.

APRIL

# 17

Bring in the Light

Most people don't feel motivated in dark spaces because darkness signals to your body that you should be resting and sleeping, which disrupts your circadian rhythm.

As a means of self-care, light up your room today. Open the windows, turn on the lights, bring even more sources of light into your room, or go outside for a 10-minute walk in the sunshine.

APRIL

# 18

~

## Roll It Out

Your muscles respond to direct pressure by relaxing. Any pressure applied to your superficial muscles penetrates, in a ripple effect, the deeper muscle layers as well, reducing your body's inflammation and creating a general calming environment in your body.

You can care for your muscles by rolling them out. If you don't have a foam roller, use any large, firm cylindrical or round object you have at home (such as a thermos or tennis ball). Starting at your feet, roll in long passes up and down your legs and arms, feeling a relaxing wave wash over your muscles.

APRIL

# 19

~

*I am awesome. I am moving forward. I am succeeding. I am strong. I am powerful. I am one of a kind. I don't try to be what I am not. I am me!*

## 20

# Big Reward

Start planning the dream trip that you've always wanted to take. Whether it's been a matter of money, time off from work, being away from your family, or the sense that you don't deserve a break that's been holding you back, allow yourself to move slowly toward your dream. Regardless if it will happen next month, next year, or even years from now, the time has come to set the plan in motion. Choose where you want to go, pick a date, and start planning and saving. Whenever the day-to-day leaves you feeling discouraged or stressed, remember that your dream trip is truly on the horizon.

APRIL

# 21

~

## Read and Listen

If you are struggling in any way with willpower and motivation, know that you can and will overcome it. Willpower is a muscle to be strengthened, like any other. Invest in yourself today by looking for resources—such as self-help books, podcasts, websites, or the counsel of a mentor or friend—that will help you build and flex your willpower muscles. You can do it!

APRIL

# 22

~

## Dress to Impress

Sometimes, paying close attention to your clothes or appearance can feel superficial. But there are very real psychological effects that come from what you wear. According to research, formal wear can increase your sense of confidence and make you a better negotiator. (Yes, they research this stuff!) Experiment with wearing clothes that make you feel assured, strong, and pow- erful. Whether it's a gown in the back of your closet or a three-piece suit, try it on and see how you feel.

# 23

~~

## Find a Time to Rest

There is a time to push and a time to rest. Your life is a journey, and you are in it for the long haul. This is a beautiful and hopeful truth because you need a balance of inhaling and exhaling. Inhaling looks like discipline, motivation, productivity, work, and life maintenance. Exhaling is relaxation, quiet time, play, and laughter. Know yourself well enough to recognize your limits. Be good to yourself today by finding moments of rest.

May you inhale and exhale deeply and regularly.

# 24

## Know Your Strengths

Do you solemnly swear to stay in your lane, your whole lane, and nothing but your lane?

The biggest motivation killer is comparison. Reflect on how you compare yourself with others. Sometimes when you make choices as a direct result of comparing yourself with someone else, you fail at your goals or intentions because you are trying to occupy a lane of life that isn't your own. Your lane is made just for you, and it's beautiful just the way it is. Feel good about staying in your lane—it's where all your potential and passions lie. When you focus on your own lane, you can appreciate your unique growth.

## 25

# Fake It 'til You Become It

The concept of "faking it until you become it" may sound, well, fake on its own, but there's real power in this way of thinking. The concept supports the cognitive behavioral theory of healthy self-motivation and mental health. Just like laughing increases your mood, imitating confidence, competence, and positivity allows you to truly nurture those qualities.

Today, if you aren't feeling motivated, pretend that you are. Tell yourself how energized you feel about presenting that project at work or how pumped you are for your workout today. The more you practice aspirational self-talk, the more it will become truth.

# 26

## Dust Yourself Off and Start Again

When you fall, dust yourself off and start all over again. How do you do this? The best way is to prepare for making a mistake before you do. Create a short list of methods and phrases that you can apply in a caring way when your motivation or self-confidence is low because you messed up. Think of encouraging words or actions that you would offer to a friend in need of a confidence boost and some forgiveness. Give them to yourself, as necessary.

# 27

## Consider Criticism Carefully

Always consider criticism—if it isn't an obvious direct, personal attack. You can learn a great deal about yourself from how people perceive you and your words. But you must care for yourself by guarding what type of criticism you take in. Considering what someone has to say is not the same as absorbing it as your truth. Examine the life of the person who is critiquing you. Do they have value to offer? Be intentional about how you react to criticism, too. Don't respond immediately, but only after careful consideration. Use vetted critiques as a tool for improvement.

# 28

## No More Waiting

You may often compromise your needs, wants, and desires by putting things off: *Wait until the kids get older. Wait until I lose the weight. Wait until I make more money. Wait until I truly fall in love.*

You are perfect enough just the way you are, and there is no need to wait. You are given one life, and you are guaranteed only this present moment.

Do something or start a project today that you've been putting off. You've got this!

# 29

## Write Your Own Pep Talk

Gift your mind an opportunity to rendezvous with positivity as you go about your day by jotting down some of your favorite motivational quotes and hanging them somewhere conspicuous. Every time you see them, it'll feel like a chance encounter with love, motivation, and self-care.

APRIL

# 30

## Give Yourself a Hand

Write down all the positive changes you have effected in your life that were difficult to do. Applaud yourself for your effort, strength, and bravery. Reflect on how much better your life is today because of the hard choices you made.

Focus on releasing the least beneficial aspects of yourself and multiplying the healthy.

# Simplicity

## Be like a tree and let the dead leaves drop.

—RUMI

This month is all about simplicity. When you are committed to simplifying your life, your priorities, desires, and deep needs rise to the surface. When life is cluttered with things and busyness, you become blind to your needs. The complex demands of the day-to-day grind overshadow the more important, simple needs of your life.

Sometimes you may hold on to possessions, relationships, people, and ideas long after their expiration date. It's okay—necessary even—to let the things, people, and feelings that you no longer need fall away. When you remove the old to make way for the new, you are simply acknowledging what is and what isn't in your life.

Simplifying gives you the necessary space to breathe in deeply. It feeds your soul and creativity, and it allows you to lead an empowered life.

# 1

## Choose One

Think of one habit that isn't benefiting you. Do you eat when you're stressed? Are you a smoker? A nail-biter? Whatever that bad habit is, let it go this month.

But don't quit the habit without replacing it with an alternative. Your habitual choices serve the purpose of fulfilling a need—sometimes in a healthy way, sometimes in an unhealthy way. Consider the need itself and how you can replace it with a healthier choice that will fulfill you.

# 2

## Unfollow Negativity

Unfollow or mute anyone on social media whose presence and opinions feel in conflict with your soul. If they don't bring you joy, or otherwise uplift you, do not give them any attention or valuable real estate in your life.

~

## Simplify Routines

Routines can feel monotonous, but they simplify your life while increasing productivity. Morning and bedtime routines are especially important. Make them simple, but reproducible daily, based on your priorities. Establishing routines makes transitions easier and creates less stress on your body, allowing you to accomplish more than when you haphazardly attend to your priorities.

~

## Forgive Yourself

Write down everything for which you need to forgive yourself. Read the list, then rip it into tiny pieces and throw them in the trash. Tell yourself, *I am forgiven!*

**The simple things are also the most extraordinary things, and only the wise can see them.**

—PAULO COELHO

## Slow It Down

The pressures of life seem to create a mandate that you do more to keep up. Identify one place in your life where you need to do the opposite and slow down. What can you put into practice? Who can you call on for assistance so that you can slow down in this area?

**The key is not to prioritize what's on your schedule, but to schedule your priorities.**

—STEPHEN COVEY

## Ask Yourself

What choices distract you from caring for yourself? Remember that it's not the people you love in your life that keep you from caring for yourself, rather it's the behaviors you choose that take precedence over your own health. How can you adjust, let go of, elicit help for, or change those behaviors to make more space for you? Don't accept "I can't" as an answer. Think about it today and take comfort knowing that you deserve an answer.

## Toss It Out

Your closet is not a museum. Let your journals, pictures, and memories tell the stories of days gone by, not your clothes, shoes, and accessories. Today, declutter your wardrobe. If you didn't wear something at all last season, donate it. Instead of owning an overabundant wardrobe, get rid of the clutter. What you have is enough, and if you need to, slowly replace your wardrobe with quality pieces that make you feel good and inspired to dress for your beautiful life.

**Minimalism isn't about removing the things you love; it's about removing the things that distract you from the things you love.**

—JOSHUA BECKER

# 11

## Set Yourself Free

If you feel like you're being held prisoner with negative emotions because of something someone did to you, take steps to forgive them. This forgiveness is a gift to your current and future self, creating ripple effects in all your relationships.

Remember that forgiveness doesn't mean you excuse bad behavior; it means you choose healing for yourself.

# 12

## Unsubscribe from the Unnecessary

You are responsible for guarding your time and energy. Unsubscribe from email lists that create distraction and suck up unnecessary seconds of your day. It may seem small, but it makes a substantial difference to never have to manage emails from that list again. You are prioritizing your time and setting your boundaries.

# 13

**A walk in nature walks the soul back home.**

—ECKHART TOLLE

# 14

## You Simply Matter

Meditate on the vastness of the world. Remember that you are part of a larger whole, and although you belong to a wide tapestry of life, the reality of your very existence is in fact so beautifully uncomplicated. You are here. You matter. It is that wonderfully simple.

# 15

## Simplify Your Beauty

Cosmetic companies would have you believe that you need a different product for every inch of your body. How can you simplify your regimen? Consider removing one step in your routine today. Wait a few weeks, then evaluate whether the change made a difference. You may find that you can remove a few steps and still maintain the same results.

MAY

# 16

## Check Your Priorities

What are your highest priorities? Write them down. Now, evaluate how you spend your days. Are your daily activities reflective of your priority list? If not, consider eliminating items that aren't so that you can live the life you want.

~~

## Limit How You Communicate

Sometimes you may feel so obligated to stay connected that you overwhelm yourself with technology that was supposed to make your life easier. There are unlimited and demanding vehicles for communication—texts, emails, DMs, voice mails, and Facebook Messenger, to name a few. From now on, engage with only the method(s) of communication that work best for you and make you feel connected. Don't worry about being out of touch by not using all of the methods. Let your people know how they can interact with you. By simplifying, you'll be an even better communicator.

MAY

# 18

~~

**As I unclutter my life, I free myself to answer the callings of my soul.**

—WAYNE DYER

# 19

## Clear Your Desktop

A disorganized computer desktop is just as distracting and draining as a chaotic workspace or living space. Organize your desktop files into helpful folders so that the files are easy to find. You will work faster with less frustration when you don't waste valuable time looking for a file.

# 20

## Do What Dogs Do

Imagine you're a wonderfully pampered house dog and take 15 minutes to indulge in behaving like one without a care in the world. Lie around, eat and drink at your leisure, seek out a comforting pat, and see what other relaxing activities you can get into. It's a simple, carefree life. Enjoy it!

## 21

~

## Gentle Is the New Perfect

Take a few minutes today to remember to be gentle with yourself. The world isn't going to stop rotating if you don't get everything done. Move forward with grace for yourself. In all your imperfections, you are beautiful.

MAY

## 22

~

## The first step in crafting a life you want is to get rid of everything you don't.

—JOSHUA BECKER

# 23

~

## Keep Your Mind Clean

A cluttered mind is distracted, forgetful, and generally overwhelmed. Consider purging your thoughts into a Notes folder on your tablet or phone today. Do this regularly with anything on your mind that you can't take care of in the moment. Remind yourself that you have recorded it and don't need to hold it in your thoughts anymore—it will be there when you are ready to tackle it. Take a deep breath and enjoy your uncluttered mind.

MAY

# 24

~

## Vent It Out

Venting and complaining are fraternal twins. There is health in venting, but very little of it in complaining. Vent to a trusted friend, your journal, or a voice recorder.

Purging your thoughts deepens your understanding of yourself. Sometimes you don't know how you truly feel until you talk or write it out.

~

## Beauty Consumer

Surrounding yourself with beauty is a simple method of self-care. Beauty calms and heals the spirit. Hospital patients who have a window with a view of nature heal faster and are discharged sooner than those who don't. Listen to beautiful music, hang that beautiful picture that's been sitting in your closet, or go on a nature walk and notice the beauty in creation. Do something today to intentionally consume beauty.

~

**The great benefit of slowing down is reclaiming the time and tranquility to make meaningful connections— with people, with culture, with work, with nature, with our own bodies and minds.**

—CARL HONORÉ

MAY

## 27

# Open Your Calendar

Scrutinize your calendar for the upcoming weeks. What commitment is a waste of your time—time that could be spent better by doing something that really matters to you? Once you identify the activity, cancel it. It may feel uncomfortable at first to let go of an obligation—personal or professional—but the benefit of creating space for what's important to you far outweighs a brief moment of discomfort. This is you caring for yourself.

MAY

## 28

# Save the Trees

Eliminate stress caused by large amounts of paperwork. Be kind to yourself by getting rid of any paperwork that isn't absolutely necessary. Shift account statements and notifications to online.

# 29

It is the simple things of life that make living worthwhile, the sweet fundamental things such as love and duty, work and rest, and living close to nature.

—LAURA INGALLS WILDER

# 30

*I am uncluttering my life and freeing myself to connect with my soul.*
*I am finding peace in simplifying my life.*
*I am finding joy in ordinary moments.*
*I am embracing simplicity because it enriches my life.*

~~

## Ask Yourself, What Else?

You have come to the end of the month of simplicity. I encourage you to maintain a regular practice of letting go of anything that no longer serves you. Anytime you carry out a simple task of release—something as mundane as taking out the recycling—ask yourself, *What else do I need to let go of in my life?*

You are letting go of anything that no longer serves you or your purpose in life.

# Encouragement

**If you don't like something, change it; if you can't change it, change the way you think about it.**

—MARY ENGELBREIT

Welcome to June! The sixth month of the year is the perfect check-in point for your self-care journey and the optimal season for additional encouragement. You've edited out some unnecessary items and habits from your life to prioritize your own well-being, so now you can focus on encouraging your spirit.

The medial prefrontal cortex is a region of the brain that essentially sits between your eyes. It's the region most associated with self-processing and is activated when a person reflects on themselves—much like you are doing now, as you work your way through this book, and especially in the month of June. Place your finger on the space between your eyes and send it some loving and caring thoughts. You matter.

JUNE

# 1

## Shower Yourself

Shower yourself with words of comfort like raindrops: *I am a beautiful butter-fly, unfolding into my greatest potential.*

JUNE

# 2

## Open Gratitude

Return to the gratitude jar that you've been contributing to since January. It's okay if you haven't been adding to it every day. Empty the contents and read what you have been thankful for since the beginning of the year. Lean into the feeling of gratitude, taking inspiration from how it has grown over the months. When you are finished, return the contents to the jar. Continue to keep up the habit of adding to the jar each day if you can. You are creating a gift for yourself.

JUNE

# 3

## Spin It!

Try to reframe the memories of past negative events over which you have no control. When you view your experiences through a negative lens, even if they were challenging or upsetting incidents, it creates a melancholy mental blanket that weighs you down. Reframing negative thought lifts that blanket and tenderly cares for your mind.

Flip the script and move through your day with this new outlook.

JUNE

# 4

~

## Find Your Joy

Today, focus on cultivating joy. You may have to search for it, but some-where inside of you lives a spark of joy. It's what keeps you alive, it's what gets you out of bed in the morning, and it's what pushed you to embark on a self-care journey.

Sometimes you may get bogged down by all the things that feel wrong in your life. The perfect, simplest solution can be to look up, turn your face toward the sun, and acknowledge all that is good.

JUNE

# 5

~

*I am offering the best of myself every day. Perfection is not required. I am letting go of yesterday and am present in this day. I have the power to create my tomorrows.*

# 6

~~

## Walk Unassisted

Leave your cell phone at home and take a walk. Notice how much more of the world you experience with your head up and without the distractions of a screen or music. Encourage yourself with this affirmation:

*I am my own superhero. I am in charge of how I experience the world and I choose to see it through a lens of happiness.*

# 7

~

## Meditate Much?

### Quiet the mind and the soul will speak.

—MA JAYA SATI BHAGAVATI

Meditation can be an intimidating, if not downright frustrating, experience for many people. *I'm not doing it right, I fall asleep, and I can't clear my mind* are common responses for people beginning a practice of meditation.

Clearing your mind is not a requirement for meditation. There is no right way to do it—even if you fall asleep. Meditating is about getting still with yourself, being curious, and accepting and becoming acquainted with your thoughts. Start with just two minutes today. Simply sit and be still.

## Be Flawsome

Consider your biggest flaw. Acknowledge why it bothers you. Search deeply to see if there are issues that you may need to work on. Banish the fantasy of how much better your life would be without it.

Find strength in your flaw. You can embrace a blemish and work on improving it at the same time. You are a unique snowflake. Being the same is overrated (and impossible).

## Release a Little Self-Esteem

When you seek the approval of others, you risk demoralizing yourself. You are essentially saying, *Their opinion about me is more important than my opinion about myself.* Care for yourself today by validating who you are.

*I don't expect everyone to approve of me. My value is based on what I think of myself. My self-esteem is mine alone.*

# 10

## Change Is Beautiful

Life never ceases to hide a surprise around the corner. Some freeze in fear at the thought of change. Instead, try to embrace the certainty that it is. Focus on loving every second of your life. Allow yourself to grieve change that you really don't want to happen, with the knowledge that you also don't want to go back to your former life, either.

There are so many gifts in this moment and up ahead for you. If you have difficulty with change, care for yourself today by embracing it:

*I am good with change. I bring myself with me to every new season. I comfort myself through the process of change. I am excitedly open to new beginnings.*

# 11

## Find Your Color

The impact of beauty on your psyche is enormous. Some may view beauty as a frivolous or peripheral part of the world. It most certainly is not. Beauty is a human necessity, and nature is beauty epitomized. Beauty exists in the vast array of colors you encounter each day. Certain colors resonate deeply with different people. The right color seems to perfectly match the song in your soul. Identify your color today. Is it deep blue? Vibrant yellow? Dusky red? Commit to surround yourself with more of your favorites.

# 12

## Observe the Birds

Stand under the shade of the largest tree that you can find and look up. You are a part of the beauty that is in the world. Bird-watch today. Listen to their music and remind yourself how well you are taken care of. Remember, you are valuable and loved. You are well cared for. And you love yourself above all.

# 13

## Be Your Very Best Friend

Treat yourself like you would a friend. Walk with yourself through your uneasiness. Don't rush to the next thing. Listen intently. Nod in understanding. Hold your own hand and say, *I understand. I see you and hear you.* You are doing a great job! I am here for you.

# 14

## Reward Yourself

Pat yourself on the back for your hard work this month. It's not indulgent to acknowledge your accomplishments. It's you taking care of you.

Today, decide on an encouraging reward. Give it to yourself, then state aloud the accomplishment for which you are rewarding yourself. Tell yourself that you are doing a good job. Honor how hard you are working and remember that your pace is good enough.

# 15

## Gut Love

A healthy gut protects you from disease, keeps inflammation low, and even promotes mental health.

Focus on your gut health today. Avoid foods that aren't healthy for your gut bacteria, such as artificial sweeteners, processed foods, and sugary foods. Try something new that feeds a healthy gut, such as fermented foods or those loaded with probiotics, including sauerkraut, asparagus, and kimchi.

# 16

## Try Naked Feet

Walking barefoot, known as earthing, can be a form of healing. When your bare skin connects with the grass, your nerves synchronize your body with the earth's natural electric charge, creating changes in the electrical activity in your brain.

So much of the day is spent touching artificial, manufactured objects. Instead, try touching the earth today to connect your spirit with nature.

JUNE

# 17

*I am taking good care of myself, and I would not have it any other way.*

JUNE

# 18

## Just Dance

What was your favorite song in high school? Play it and dance to it. Nostalgic practices regulate mood, creating an overall sense of well-being. Dancing increases cognitive processing and reduces anxiety. And don't forget to sing out loud!

# 19

## Puzzled

Start a puzzle today. The quiet concentration required to complete a puzzle is a wonderful stress reliever. You are utilizing your visual/spatial reasoning to match the pieces, but the quiet also allows space for your mind to breathe and process.

# 20

## You're Responsible

Take responsibility for, and pride in, your adult life. Remind yourself that whatever may have happened during your childhood is not your fault, but it is your duty to heal now. It is also your obligation to take responsibility for your part in every relationship or situation as an adult. Ask yourself, *What was my part? How can I change it?*

The beautiful thing about responsibility is that it gives you the power. You have the power to change your life once you acknowledge your part in it.

JUNE

# 21

~

## Resist the Urge to Move

Self-care is about finding the balance between what you need to do and what you want to do. Making time for stillness when your internal drive is propelling you to busyness calms the mind and allows you to focus. Let go of the urgency and sit in five minutes of silence.

JUNE

# 22

~

## Begin to Heal

What part of you needs to heal? Unhealed wounds don't always cause noticeable pain, but they do cause weariness because of the subconscious, emotional energy needed to tend to them. This excessive drag makes living a little harder. Numbing your pain with distraction, bad habits, and secret obsessions are just flimsy Band-Aids.

Although your pain won't be eliminated today, you can begin the process by purchasing a book, scheduling a session with a therapist, reading an article, journaling, or sharing your hurt with a trusted friend. Start healing that wound.

# Nonnegotiable

Self-care is neither a luxury nor a reward. It is not a privilege. Self-care is a necessity for healthy living. Be nonnegotiable about the time and space your self-care encompasses. Above all, give yourself what you need.

# Treasure Your Body

Your body is amazing! Loving it for all that it is, and all that it gives you, is the ultimate form of self-care. Pay attention to all the quirky, unique, and mundane things your body can do. Create a list of what your body is capable of. Read it aloud and be thankful for your life's vehicle. Embrace and love your body. It's the most amazing gift you will ever own.

## 25

# Scan Your Body

To care for yourself properly, you must be deeply acquainted with yourself. Slowing down to listen to your body's language helps you develop deep compassion and understanding for yourself. A powerful way to connect with your body is through a mindfulness "body scan" exercise.

Lie flat on a bed, mat, or rug. Breathe slowly in and out, focusing all your attention on the top of your head. How does your headspace feel? Do you feel the hard floor or soft pillow underneath you? Are you experiencing any twinges, tingles, or pain? Slowly work your way down your body until you get to your feet. Just observe and notice. Get to know yourself.

# 26

## Unshould

Consider the word should and its impact on your sense of well-being. It may seem like a motivating word, but actually it is encoded deeply in your emotional programming through outside influences, and it probably isn't supportive or encouraging. Walking down the "should" path often leads to struggle and disappointment. Shoulds interrupt your present by suggesting what you're currently doing is not enough, creating needless guilt and angst.

Let go of an unreasonable obligation by examining what you want. When shoulds disrupt your peace, ask yourself, Do I want this? Why? Use the words want and need as a replacement and see if they feel more congruous.

# 27

## Dress with Care

Dress your body like it is a piece of art. Be purposeful, intentional, and expressive. Choose clothes that make your body feel good. When you adorn your body intentionally, you are sending a message to yourself and the world that this is a person well cared for—and feeling well cared for increases your desire to actually continue to care for yourself.

JUNE

# 28

## Selfie Work

Take a photo of yourself as you are in this moment. Observe the image and give love to the person looking back at you. Talk to them. Encourage them: *I'm looking clearly at myself with my own eyes. I am processing the feelings that come up for me when I look at myself. I modify scripts in my mind that say I am not good enough. I am enough.*

# 29

## Do New

Do something new with your body. Your mind becomes numb to the same repeated stimulation every day. Awaken your senses by doing something new today. Try a different exercise outside of your comfort zone. Dance or swim naked. Explore what the world has to offer.

JUNE

# 30

**Self-love is respecting my beautiful body. Yes, it is beautiful! It was divinely designed especially for me. A sacred creation . . . which brings me limitless opportunities to experience myself in each moment.**

—MICHELLE McGRATH

# Purpose

**The two most important days in life are the day you were born and the day you discover why.**

—MARK TWAIN

Your purpose is the reason for which you were created. Your purpose is the highest expression of your abilities. Care for yourself this month by diving a little deeper into discovering your greatest talents. Embark on an internal treasure hunt and discover how you can show up in the most caring way for yourself as you offer your very best gifts to the world.

Purpose assigns a meaning to all that you do. You connect to your purpose by looking inward, where everything important always is.

# 1

## Stay in Your Lane

It's far too easy to find thousands of reasons to believe that you aren't enough. But you are more than enough. Your viewpoint, experiences, and manner of expressing them to the world are precisely what this universe needs. Comparison will compromise your soul. You are in a lane that is not supposed to look like anyone else's. Your lane is perfectly made for you.

# 2

## It's Never Too Late to Learn

Learn something new. Register for an academic class at a local college, sign up for online lessons in an area that piques your interest, or join a local community group that practices an activity you've never tried before. Taking a variety of classes is the best way to explore possibilities of interests and talents.

JULY

# 3

The meaning of life is to find your gift. The purpose of life is to give it away.

—PABLO PICASSO

JULY

# 4

## Stop Seeking the Temporary

If your greatest focus is on self-pleasure, then you may be creating a recipe for self-absorption and chronic unhappiness. Self-care is always nurturing, but not always pleasurable. The goal is to have a well-cared-for mind, body, and spirit. Self-care also creates room to give, once you yourself have been filled. Happiness is temporary and centered around something outside of yourself. A sense of well-being is internal and long-lasting. When you pursue care, not temporary happiness, you can rest assured that contentment will follow.

# 5

*I choose to take actions that are in alignment with my purpose. I let go of anything that isn't mine to pursue.*

# 6

## Think Short

Sometimes finding purpose isn't a massive, long-term, overarching excavation of your life. You can find purpose in the next choice, decision, or right step. Choices piled on top of choices create a life. You are finding purpose in the beautiful monotony of every day. Each day, you get to make a choice that brings you closer to the exquisite expression of your purpose on earth.

# 7

~

## Do Life in the Real World

Engage in purposeful human-to-human interaction today. You create a false sense of community when you connect with your people predominantly through devices. There is a restorative energy that exists between two people experiencing eye contact and being in proximity to each other. Set a date to meet a friend in person today.

JULY

# 8

~

## Remember

Take a trip in your mind's eye back to your childhood. What made the hours rush by like wind? Social pressures and ideas about how you "should be" can squeeze the passion out of you. You may often disregard your childish desires and obsessions. Rediscovering what you loved as a child is usually the key to unlocking your purpose. As a child, you were purely connecting with yourself, unfiltered. Travel back and see how you can incorporate those enjoyable experiences into your present life and multiply them.

*Every day, I feel a greater sense of excitement, anticipation, and peace as I further align with my purpose.*

## Deep Listening

Listening to someone else is the most simple and powerful way to connect. You can also connect deeply with yourself by listening.

Speak to yourself out loud today. Listen to your tone, inflections, energy, and mood. Now think deeply about who you are. What are your deepest desires, fears, and insecurities? How can you support yourself?

# 11

## Who?

Knowing yourself deeply is a powerful way to care for yourself. You may go about life believing what you have been taught without a solid understanding of why.

If you are unaware of your values, then you are essentially living out other people's values and priorities instead of your own.

Ask yourself hard questions:

*Why do I believe what I believe? How do I know it to be true?*

# 12

## Be of Service

Being of service to others is a powerful antidepressant. Give to yourself today by becoming a helper. Look for opportunities to help. Those who serve the most, reap the most.

# 13

## Share Your Story

Everyone has a unique life experience and perspective that highlights global truths about the world.

Own your story in the most magnificent way. Share it with a friend, a colleague, a family member, or even a stranger. Help someone who may have had a similar journey. Sharing your story heals your inner child, your adult self, your future children, and anyone else who needs to hear it.

# 14

*I know my purpose will continue to unfold and be revealed to me as I honor its existence and trust in my ability to fulfill it.*

# 15

~

## Espresso-less

Consider reducing your caffeine intake. Caffeine stimulates stress hormones, increasing fight-or-flight responses. Cutting back on caffeine can lower your blood pressure, increase your absorption of nutrients, decrease anxiety, and increase your sense of peace. Be kind to your body by cutting back slowly.

# 16

~

## Fix the Wrong

Once basic needs are cared for, the human psyche begins to seek a deeper meaning in life. Humans with a clear sense of purpose tend to live longer, enjoying better health and an overall sense of well-being. One way to explore your purpose is to consider injustices that bother you. Think about how you can participate in positive change in that area—whether it's through a full-time pursuit or part-time donation of your time.

# 17

The purpose of life is not to be happy. It is to be useful, to be honorable, to be compassionate, to have it make some difference that you have lived and lived well.

—RALPH WALDO EMERSON

# 18

## Elevator Pitch

In less than 100 words, write out your life's philosophy. Consider framing it and placing it somewhere central and visible. This is your personal mission statement, and you can refer to it when you are feeling lost.

# 19

*I am able to walk on my own unique path, looking neither beside me nor behind me, knowing that this path was made for me, and I am here on purpose.*

# 20

## Consume Purposefully

Today, ask your body how it feels after everything you've consumed—for example, the food you ate and the media you absorbed. Ask how you can better nourish your body.

Speak this affirmation: *I am the gatekeeper for my mind, body, and spirit. Through my diligent guarding, I maintain my health.*

# 21

## Listen Up!

## He who knows others is wise; he who knows himself is enlightened.

—LAO TZU

You have varied passions and talents. You probably discount the things that come easy for you because you possess the idea that a purpose must be hard won and complicated. It doesn't need to be. If you are having a difficult time determining your purpose, ask the trusted people in your life where they think your talents lie. They should be able to provide insight because they don't devalue your gifts. Take note of the compliments you receive. They are clues about your strengths.

JULY

# 22

*I tell myself only the things that I want to come true in my life. I think my future into existence while I honor and live in the present.*

# 23

## Talk to Strangers

The next time you are standing in a line, make a concerted effort not to use your phone to pass the time. Instead, strike up a conversation with the person next to you. If this feels awkward, that's okay. You are stretching yourself and growing. Engaging with people outside of your regular social circle exposes you to ideas and activities you may never have considered before, and it could lead you closer to discovering your purpose.

JULY

# 24

**It takes courage to grow up and become who you really are.**

—E.E. CUMMINGS

# 25

## Scream It Out

Primal screams are a productive way to purge negative emotion. Release any frustrations, anger, sadness, or rage—emotions that can block your ability to walk in your purpose.

Find the thickest pillow in your home, take a deep breath, and scream loudly into it. Keep screaming until you run out of steam. Take some cleansing deep breaths when you are finished and notice how much lighter you feel.

# 26

*I know what I want out of life, and life gives it to me. I am allowing my purpose to scream louder than my doubt.*

## 27

# Become an Explorer

Be open to new experiences. The more things you are willing to try, the happier and more fulfilling your life becomes and the more likely you are to discover your purpose. The fewer things you are willing to try, the more immobilized you become. Being open is a caring and exciting way to live your life.

*I am open to new things. I am willing to take a leap between familiarity and the unknown.*

## 28

# Compose Your Obituary

Write your obituary with love, gratitude, and hope. This may seem macabre, but there is so much to gain from thinking about what legacy you want to leave in this world. Your obituary should be a celebration of your life. Honor what you have done and what you still intend to do in this world.

# 29

*My purpose propels me at exactly the right speed. Life isn't about quickly arriving at the completion of my purpose; it's about the route along the way.*

# 30

## An Affirmation Just for You

Make a list of qualities and habits you'd like to develop. You've just written your own personal affirmations.

Replace the beginning of each sentence with this: *I Am . . .*

# 31

~

## The World Needs You

As you end this month of purpose, take a moment to pause and consider your path. Are your daily activities taking you in the direction that you want to go? If not, you can always double back and begin anew. Sometimes the road to finding your purpose is meandering. Every pause and fork in the road are a part of the plan.

The world needs your unique magic. Perhaps being yourself in this world is your purpose. Show up as your true self. There is no one else like you.

# Discipline

**Discipline is built by consistently performing small acts of courage.**

—ROBIN SHARMA

Self-care is not an occasional indulgence, rather it is a discipline—an intentional choice to care for your future self. People who possess discipline have a better sense of well-being and a greater sense of control over their life because they are not ruled by impulses. Taking full and complete responsibility for your well-being requires discipline. *Discipline* is a magnificent word that bequeaths freedom to the beholder.

Focus this month on the beauty that is the practice of discipline.

Self-discipline equals self-care.

AUGUST

# 1

*I am strong. I can change my habits easily. I have the wisdom and courage to create systems that propel me toward the life I want.*

AUGUST

# 2

## Remove Temptations

Remove distracting or damaging temptations from your environment. Temptations create stress, even when you resist them. Your home should be a welcoming, freeing space for your spirit, where your routines flow.

# 3

〜

**Discipline yourself to do the things you need to do when you need to do them, and the day will come when you will be able to do the things you want to do when you want to do them.**

—ZIG ZIGLAR

# 4

## Give Yourself Goose Bumps

Create goose bumps on your skin. This may seem like an odd trick, but this ability demonstrates your mind's power to influence systems in your body. There is nothing subtle about the connection between your mind and your physical self. Creating goose bumps is a process whereby you get closer to your body.

Close your eyes and take two deep breaths. Focus on the sensation of your skin. Allow your mind to think of all the amazing possibilities in your life. Think about the surprising contrasts and ironies you've experienced. Feel the goose bumps rise. Look at your skin, and marvel at the power you have to influence yourself.

AUGUST

# 5

*I am walking in my purpose with strength and excitement. I love what I have to offer the world. I enjoy honing my craft. I am a flaming ball of opportunity.*

# 6

## Change Your Perception

Willpower sounds like a harsh practice of excessive restriction that you are struggling to uphold. Although self-discipline may seem like basic willpower, viewing it that way doesn't work because shame over inevitable backslides will reduce your ability to stay on course. Willpower and discipline pair well together—you can't have one without the other—but you have to view them correctly. If you see delayed gratification as necessary to create something better in your life, you will succeed. Believe you are not restricting, but rather giving yourself a gift.

# 7

*I exercise because it makes my body feel good to be fit. I eat my greens because it feels good in my body when I eat healthy food. I go to sleep early because it feels good to wake up rested. I tell the truth because the truth is freeing.*

# 8

~

## Never Ask Yourself...

Never ask yourself if you feel up to doing a hard workout, waking up to an early-morning alarm, or having a difficult conversation. Rather, once you've decided to proceed with an action, go forward without hesitation, trusting that you can do it. Tell yourself, *I know why I have chosen this for my life. I am honoring that choice and I'm proud of myself.*

AUGUST

# 9

~

**True self-care is not salt baths or chocolate cake, it is making the choice to build a life you don't need to regularly escape from.**

—BRIANNA WIEST

# 10

## Sleep Appointment

Make a calendar appointment for your bedtime. Restorative sleep creates more productivity in your waking hours. You may believe that staying up late to get work done or enjoy "you" time is taking care of yourself, but it isn't. The result is exhaustion and reduced performance in the following days.

Avoid harsh transitions before sleep. Instead, choose to quit working or looking at a screen an hour before bedtime. Create a transition activity that allows your mind to switch off and peacefully drift to sleep.

# 11

~~

## **Turn Habits into Destiny**

Goals and dreams are crucial, but unattainable without habits attached to them. Write down or revisit your list of goals. For each goal, outline a behavior associated with attaining that goal that you already are integrating or will incorporate into your schedule on a regular basis. Do you want to write a book? How often and when will you write regularly? Do you want to get in shape? How will you fit your workouts and eating changes into your lifestyle? Being intentional about how you will accomplish your goals is what transforms dreams into destiny.

# 12

## Money Smart

Write down your monetary goals—such as paying off debt or saving for a home—and the small sacrifices needed to achieve them. Taking good financial care of yourself includes having the discipline to live within your means and save a little something from every paycheck for emergencies and retirement.

Start with a plan for eliminating your unsecured debt, then once it's paid off, allocate that same money toward savings. Consider a separate bank account for each of your major savings goals.

AUGUST

# 13

## Unsabotage

If you find yourself indulging in unhealthy habits and telling yourself, I deserve this, recognize that this is self-sabotage, not self-care. You don't deserve anything that isn't good for you. Even if it feels good in the moment.

*I deserve to be well taken care of. I deserve to be healthy, and I love myself enough to avoid the things that don't provide that for me.*

AUGUST

# 14

~

## Be Accountable

There is a saying that you are a combination of the five people with whom you spend the most time. Consider your circle of influence. Do those people reflect the person you want to become? Do they help create health, or do they drag down your mood or distract you from your priorities?

Accountability can be a powerful tool to assist your resolve to make healthy changes, inside and out. Consider starting an accountability group with your close friends around a similar goal. In this endeavor, you are deepening your relationships with like-minded people and strengthening your personal motivation—a double win for self-care.

# 15

You are strong when you know your weaknesses. You are beautiful when you appreciate your flaws. You are wise when you learn from your mistakes.

—UNKNOWN

# 16

## Finish What You Started

What haven't you finished? Maybe it was an exciting project that became more time-consuming than you thought it would be. Maybe it struck an emotional chord that you would rather ignore. When you leave things hanging, you create stress. Even if you think about the unfinished task only every now and then, those moments trigger a rush of emotions and negative self-talk that leave a mental hangover. Whatever the project is, take a step toward finishing it today. Baby steps are still movement in the right direction.

# 17

*Delaying gratification is caretaking your future self. A life of instant gratification is a recipe for misery.*

# 18

## What's Your Kryptonite?

Acknowledge your weakness. To increase discipline in your life, you must be aware of your significant stumbling blocks. Is it late-night popcorn? Asking someone for help? Procrastination? Take a moment and jot down the areas in yourself that need more attention to discipline.

AUGUST

# 19

*I am the master of my destiny. I use my time wisely and turn inward from distraction.*

AUGUST

# 20

## Say Goodbye to Temptation

Self-awareness allows you to circumvent temptation by doing things like eating before you go grocery shopping, putting your cell phone in your glove compartment, and keeping your gym bag packed and in your car. These are forward-thinking actions that avoid rash, regrettable decisions in the moment. Preparing for activities that are important to you increases the likelihood that you will accomplish them and do so with ease.

# 21

## Visualize It

Take a few minutes to daydream about the results of your self-care efforts. Visualize the benefit of doing the sometimes difficult, mundane task of caring for yourself. Brick by brick, you are constructing a strong foundation for your mental, spiritual, and physical health.

AUGUST

# 22

## Make Your Bed

It feels so good to slip into a nicely made bed at the end of a long day. Make a concerted effort to make your bed in the morning, as a means of caring for yourself at night.

# 23

*I am positive and resolved. I am a steel magnolia, strong enough to withstand the storm, but soft enough to comfort others.*

# 24

## Move First

Commit to beginning your day with movement—whether it's push-ups, yoga, a walk, or a run—to increase your alertness and sense of calm. People who exercise early tend to be more regular with their training sessions because their day hasn't gotten away from them and provided them with an excuse not to get to it. Exercising in the morning increases your energy throughout the day, and you benefit from the mood lift, knowing that you've already accomplished your workout.

## 25

# Sweet Discomfort

## Do not consider painful what is good for you.

—EURIPIDES

You have an innate drive to avoid discomfort, creating a sense of safety in the moment. Practice feeling uncomfortable. Whether that means completing an extra push-up or confronting an emotional issue, assure yourself that pain isn't the enemy.

## 26

# Embrace Yourself

No matter how disciplined you are on your best days, it's okay to acknowledge that you may not be that regimented all of the time. You are only human. The goal isn't perfection. It's an upward trajectory. You are on the journey. Give yourself grace.

# 27

## Social Fast

**My soul just can't do life at the speed of smartphones.**

—JOHN ELDREDGE

Delete social media from your phone for a week. You can still access it on your other devices, but you won't be checking as frequently. Consider how you can feed your spirit with the extra mental space.

# 28

## What Wisdom Teaches

Create the discipline of investing in your relationships. Interviews with cen-
tenarians have demonstrated that what the elderly regret most is not what
they didn't accomplish in their careers—it's not what personal goal they didn't
attain—but the ways they didn't invest in their relationships. They regretted
not giving enough time, energy, sympathy, or attention to the people they
loved. They lamented letting valued relationships go because of trivial issues.
Utilize the wisdom of those who have gone before you, making a regular habit
of investing in your relationships.

Make sure your people have a place in your calendar.

AUGUST

# 29

## Live Fully, Live Freely

Be open to newness. Resist getting stuck in a rut. Discipline doesn't mean that every day is Groundhog Day. You can be highly regimented and travel the world, living in a different place every month. You can practice a routine in any place and at any time—you take it with you. The universe has oodles of options for you: Try new food, move across the world, vacation somewhere unknown, or create your own style. A disciplined life gives you the freedom to live fully.

AUGUST

# 30

## Let Discipline Make Your Life

This month you have begun to wave the wand of discipline that turns dreams into reality. You possess the magic. Delayed gratification is the path. The minutes, hours, days, and weeks add up to a life of freedom. Know your weaknesses and get a head start on them. Round up some accountability. Love yourself and others to the best of your ability. This is exquisite self-care. You've got this!

# 31

With faith, discipline, and selfless devotion to duty, there is nothing worthwhile that you cannot achieve.

—MOHAMMED ALI JINNAH

# Boundaries

**Saying no to others is saying yes to yourself.**

—JACK CANFIELD

Welcome to your month of saying no. Seasons of *yes* are just around the corner, but to truly care for yourself, you must know and own your boundaries. Boundaries are internal—and sometimes external—lines that separate yourself and your will from someone else's. People with healthy boundaries value themselves as much as they do someone else. People with unhealthy boundaries either undervalue or overvalue themselves in comparison with others.

**A physical boundary clearly communicates:** This is how close you can get to me, and this is how much of my body I will allow you to engage with.

**A professional boundary clearly communicates:** This is how I will communicate with you, and these are my lines for connection and negotiation.

**An emotional boundary clearly communicates:** This is how deeply I will share my world and feelings with you, and this is how much of yours I will entertain.

**A personal boundary clearly communicates:** These are the actions I will tolerate in my relationships, and these are the ones I will not.

Expect people to impinge on your boundaries. Your self-care goal this month is to learn to better set and communicate your boundaries and to hold strong when others push against them.

Although boundaries may feel like a series of *noes*, every time you say no to something, you are really saying a resounding yes to yourself and any opportunities that will better serve you both in the now and in the long run.

*A boundary is not a rule that you impose on someone else. It is a line that you draw for yourself.*

# 1

~

## Self-Care Quiz

Boundaries are central to self-care. Here's a quick test to evaluate the status of the boundaries in your relationships:

1. Am I regularly doing something for someone that they can do for themselves (enabling)?

2. Am I putting their needs above my own most of the time (devaluing self)?

3. Do I justify bad behavior?

4. Do I say no, but give in to pressure?

5. Do I expect them to hold my boundaries?

6. Do I say yes and resent them afterward?

If you answered yes to more than two questions, I strongly encourage you to consider making a boundary change in your life. You have nothing to lose and everything to gain for yourself.

SEPTEMBER

# 2

~

## Get to Know Your Boundaries

Creating healthy boundaries is not an overnight process. Boundaries are often modeled to you during your childhood. You observe what behaviors parents or caregivers accept or reject and how it serves them. Think about the boundaries you currently have in place, then write down how they serve—or don't serve—you now. It may be that lax boundaries make you feel nice, agreeable, and likable, and the idea of erecting firm boundaries makes you feel cold, mean, and disliked. Your lack of firm boundaries may serve you in that people like you, but it hurts you because you give away precious time, feel unappreciated, and develop resentment as a result. The first step to change is understanding why your current patterns exist to begin with.

SEPTEMBER

# 3

~

*I understand that people will treat me as well as I demand to be treated, by what I allow, what I choose to stop, and behaviors that I reinforce.*

# 4

## The Shoulds

List all the shoulds in your life—the feelings, expectations, or obligations that someone else imposes on you. Think about who you worry about disappointing if you don't follow through on *their* desires. Write down their names next to each corresponding should. Review the list once more, crossing out the shoulds that you no longer wish to feel burdened by or allow to define you. Starting today, let go of the shoulds for good.

After you make your list, say, *I accept me all of the time in all the ways. I am allowed to be in progress.*

# 5

~

# **Set Healthy Boundaries**

As you speak clearly with an expectation to be respected, refrain from using words like *I think, I would like, I would appreciate that,* or *That would be nice.* Instead, use clear, direct phrases, communicating that a boundary is not a desire. It's a nonnegotiable.

Use these boundary setting statements as you move through your day:

> *No.*
> *That doesn't work for me.*
> *I can't help you.*
> *I'm not okay with that.*
> *If you want to be in relationship with me, this needs to change.*
> *You are asking me to do something that I don't feel comfortable with and I won't do it.*
> *I don't agree with you.*
> *Stop.*
> *This is as much as I'm willing to do.*
> *I'm not changing my mind on this.*

SEPTEMBER

# 6

*I am allowed to take up all of the space that I need. I am allowed to say all of the no's that I want. I have permission to be me all of the time in all the ways. I am allowed to be in progress.*

SEPTEMBER

# 7

## Double Down on the Good

Productivity is not the same as progress. You can complete multiple tasks for others and yourself, but if the work is not progressing you forward toward your goals, then all the effort is a practice in futility. Healthy boundaries allow you to look at what you need to cull and where you need to double down. Look at what is working in your life. You can multiply that success by letting go of what isn't working in your life.

Self-care isn't about doing better for yourself, but rather doing less of what is damaging.

# 8

*~~*

*I accept that those I love cannot fulfill all of my needs. I am responsible for my needs. I relinquish my expectation that others must take care of me.*

# 9

*~~*

## Invest Wisely

Investing in people who do not hear you, care about you, or want to learn from you is draining. As you give to your people throughout the day, ask yourself if you are people-pleasing or if you are sowing into fertile ground. People-pleasing is motivated by thoughts about how they will think of you. Sowing into fertile ground is motivated by an understanding of what you have to offer by your investment and their ability to appreciate it and/or incorporate your offering into their life in a valuable way.

SEPTEMBER

# 10

## If you want to fly, you have to give up what weighs you down.

—ROY T. BENNETT

SEPTEMBER

# 11

## Free Yourself

Sometimes you may allow people to take advantage of you simply because you love them and want to make them happy. Today, refuse to do anything for anyone else that they can do for themselves. When you consistently take care of other people's problems, you may feel that it is caring, but it is in fact enabling. When you enable someone, their growth is stunted, which prevents them from reaching their full potential.

SEPTEMBER

# 12

I have the courage to say no, even when saying yes is easier. I choose long-term ease over momentary discomfort.

SEPTEMBER

# 13

## Cost-Benefit Analysis

When deciding whether to add a new task to your to-do list, apply a cost-benefit analysis. Ask yourself, *How will this activity benefit my life? What is the (emotional, mental, or physical) cost of doing it?* Decide for yourself if the benefit is worth the cost. Honoring your time enables you to be that much more efficient in the tasks that matter, which ultimately decreases the amount of stress in your life.

SEPTEMBER

# 14

~

**Never give from the depths of your well, but from your overflow.**

—RUMI

SEPTEMBER

# 15

~

## Just Say No

Self-care through the act of creating and enforcing boundaries is not as simple as saying no to others—it's also about saying no to your own impulses that are at odds with caring for yourself. It's purposefully choosing to back-track and say no even after you've developed an intention to do something.

Tough love directed at yourself is not easy, but it's vital for your continued growth. Manage your negative impulses by choosing one harmful habit and working to reduce its importance in your life to make room for more positive thoughts and habits. Once you have conquered one habit, choose another.

# 16

~~~

## Set Your Nonnegotiables

What are the behaviors of others that you absolutely will not tolerate in your life? Write them down and place them somewhere you will come across them often—your bathroom mirror, your work desk, the kitchen fridge—to remind yourself that you won't tolerate anything less than what you really deserve.

Whenever you feel a nonnegotiable crossing your path, remind yourself:

*I love myself too much to allow these things into my life.*

# 17

## Accept Others' Limitations

A lack of boundaries can be demonstrated by overgiving, people-pleasing, and fixing, or expecting others to care for you in ways that you should be taking care of yourself.

Self-care is about taking responsibility for what is yours and not blaming others for all that's difficult in your life. The beauty of this truth is that you recognize that you have the power to create the life that you want. Often, the drive to have others take care of you comes from a need to be loved. How can you love yourself better?

## Boundary Barometer

Today, pay attention to your levels of irritation and bitterness. When you start to feel resentment, refrain from blaming someone else and check your boundaries. Resentment is the perfect barometer for measuring the health of your boundaries.

Although not making waves may smooth over situations in the moment, the resentment you build eventually seeps out, damaging the people that you love and, ultimately, yourself.

Resentment means it's time to tighten up, speak your mind, and say no. And you can verbally make your boundaries clear, with polite, quiet strength.

*I will be nice to myself. I will be easy to work with myself; I will be caring and thoughtful toward myself. From my place of happiness I will extend myself to others.*

# 20

## Build the Muscle

Do you feel butterflies in your stomach when you think of saying no to someone? Does your heart race or does your mood sink because you worry you aren't good at creating a boundary?

Setting boundaries is a muscle you must build. Work on setting an intention to say no to what doesn't serve you and your purpose. Give yourself grace for the times that you don't say no or set boundaries, and remind yourself that you are moving forward, creating a safe place to expand into your full potential. Feel that muscle grow stronger day by day.

# 21

*I understand that boundaries protect me from burnout. I uphold my boundaries internally through healthy self-talk and externally through the strong, clear words I express in interactions with others.*

# 22

*~*

## Warm Hedge

Having boundaries doesn't mean being cold, hard, and uncaring. Boundaries are not an unfeeling brick wall. As you protect your needs and limits today, visualize your boundary as a strong but soft, warm, green hedge around you. This hedge offers protection to you, but also warmth and beauty to those with whom you interact. You can quietly refuse in the kindest of ways.

# 23

*~*

**No is necessary magic. No draws a circle around you with chalk and says, "I have given enough."**

—McKAYLA ROBBIN

# 24

*I make sacrifices for those I love because I want to, not because I feel obligated, guilty, or manipulated. If I know I will resent it, I choose not to do it out of love and care for myself and others.*

# 25

## Honor Your Limits

Tangible physical boundaries are just as important as time, space, and emotional boundaries. Setting physical boundaries is a statement to yourself that you care for your body, which is valuable and deserves respect.

Honor your desire to be touched or not touched. Do not give in to another's coercion to share your personal space in any way. Every choice you make to share your body each time with those you love is your own.

SEPTEMBER

# 26

*I care for myself by assigning clear consequences for the violation of my boundaries. Boundaries don't exist without real consequences for violating them. I am the protector of my precious space.*

SEPTEMBER

# 27

## Boundary Inspiration

Think of someone who you consider has good boundaries. What actions do they take to create these boundaries? Focus on a healthy behavior that they practice—and that you admire—and replicate it as best you can. Imitation is not just flattery; it is also how you learn to apply good habits in your life.

# 28

*I am in control of how I allow others to treat me. I care for myself by guarding my boundaries. I deserve to be treated well. My wants, needs, and desires matter.*

# 29

## Boundary Show-and-Tell

Encourage someone you are in a relationship with to share the boundaries that are important to them. Listen intently. In return, share your important boundaries with them. Talk about how you can honor each other's boundaries in your relationship.

# 30

# Closing Boundary Affirmation

As you close this month of boundary setting, say these affirming words with love:

> *I give myself to those I love out of the abundance of my heart. I choose to love unconditionally, and that includes loving myself enough to say no when necessary.*

# Affirmation

## The soul should always stand ajar, ready to welcome the ecstatic experience!

—EMILY DICKINSON

Because you have culled burdensome, time-wasting tasks and relationships, you have made space for experiences, activities, and new connections that fill you up in a life-giving way. This month, I encourage you to be open to anything and everything new that underscores your self-care journey. It's important to have a balance between routine and adventure. Say yes to what lights you up!

When you say yes to an opportunity, you say yes to a new adventure. Life is meant to be lived and experienced. Remember, you are continuing to release those shoulds and unnecessary obligations. Just because you say yes today, doesn't mean that you have committed to saying yes forever. Feel free to let it flow out of your life just as easily as it arrived. It's invigorating to try new things and see what fits. Enjoy your affirming month of yes!

OCTOBER

# 1

〜

*I am an open vessel. I look forward to new things. I open the gift of life with excitement and gratitude.*

OCTOBER

# 2

〜

## Live It Up!

Plan a daring escapade that you have never tried before. This month is the perfect time to do bungee jumping, race car driving, skydiving, or a hot-air balloon ride. Not that adventurous? Try indoor skydiving, white water rafting, rock climbing, or camping overnight under the stars without a tent.

When you encounter new adventures, the emotional part of your brain that senses fear (the amygdala) lights up, causing the pleasure center of your brain (the ventral striatum) to release a jolt of excitement (dopamine), which the brain receives as a reward. Some people have longer receptors for the dopamine, making new experiences more exciting than fearful. Whichever receptor type you have, you can benefit from novel experiences and train your brain to enjoy them through repetition. Start repeating the new today!

# 3

## Ask Away

Ask as many questions as you please today. Sometimes you may censor yourself in conversations because you don't want to come across as annoying, unintelligent, or burdensome. Asking questions is a wonderful act of curiosity, engagement, and openness. You may be surprised by the new information you learn about yourself, your interests, and the ones you love through simply asking more questions.

# 4

## Say a Tiny Yes

Yeses don't have to be large in nature—or intent—to be effective. If you place a tiny yes on top of another tiny yes, they will eventually become the building blocks of a substantial life change. A tiny yes includes researching the ins and outs of a new hobby that you've been bolstering the courage to try. Say a tiny yes toward something new and exciting that you would like to implement in your life.

# 5

**Self-care is taking all of the voices of people who love you with you.**

—UNKNOWN

# 6

## Be Open

Is there a belief, idea, or stance that you have always taken that you could be open to viewing in a different way? Create space for a counterargument. Ask someone you know who has a different opinion if they can explain their point of view to you. Resist any urge to argue or feel defensive. Be open to recognizing that the way you view the world has been shaped by the lens of your specific experiences. Although you don't need to change your point of view today or ever, say yes to embracing the power of consideration. Opening yourself to understanding someone else's lens reduces fear-based judgment in yourself and allows you to defend your own beliefs more confidently on the matter.

# 7

## Do the Uncomfortable

You may find yourself admiring people who seem to walk through the world with ease and comfort in their own skin. However, for most, this takes concentrated effort and intention. What looks easy may very well be practiced. Say yes to doing the uncomfortable today to attain a feeling of confidence. It could be public speaking, wearing a bold accessory, dancing on stage—whatever it is, this act will gently push you toward growth. The sense of accomplishment, relief, and joy you feel afterward will make all the initial discomfort well worth it.

# 8

## Opposite Day

Carry out your daily activities using your nondominant hand. When you use the other hand, it is impossible to perform activities in a routine or mindless way. This tricky but rewarding experiment helps keep you centered and grounded in the present, experiencing life anew because of the attention it requires.

# 9

# Unconfirm Your Bias

Confirmation bias—not unlike the algorithms that social media uses—focuses on what you like and keeps you stuck in your ways of thinking and seeing the world. Your brain utilizes the operation of confirmation bias daily. It's too stimulating for your mind to take in every distraction in your environment. Your mind filters out what it doesn't believe is relative and focuses on what it thinks is.

Combat confirmation bias today by playing devil's advocate. Are there blue cars on the road everywhere, or is that just what you are most focused on when you observe the world around you?

# 10

# Rearrange It

Rearrange a space today. Transforming your environment sparks creativity and energizes you. Choose a space that you spend a lot of time in—such as an office, a bedroom, or a living room—and change it up. How can you make it more functional, beautiful, energizing, and new? Say yes to a space makeover.

# 11

## Learn New Tricks

What's an area of interest you haven't been willing to try because you feel like it's too late to learn? Ballet? Homeopathic medicine? Writing? Gymnastics? Robotics?

It is never too late to start something new. Take a step toward learning or pursuing a long-held interest or passion today. Silence your internal critic. Breathe through the rush of fear, and feel the excitement wash over you. Say yes because you are opening yourself up to this experience at just the right time.

OCTOBER

# 12

**Accept what people offer. Drink their milkshakes. Take their love.**

—WALLY LAMB

# 13

~~

## Open Your Heart

When you have been hurt, your natural reaction is to protect the resulting wound. You shut down, not only to heal, but also as a means of defense. In doing so, you close yourself off to loving experiences and necessary connections that bring vitality to your life. Being vulnerable is a risk worth taking. Care for yourself today by opening up to someone. Say yes to vulnerability. Push through any discomfort and share a story, explain a feeling, ask for help, or find a common ground. An open heart is a strong heart.

# 14

## Say Yes to Your Voice

Your voice is a unique gift. There is no one else in the world with a perspective like yours. When you silence yourself, you are returning your gifts unused and unappreciated. Say yes to your voice. Use it to stand up for yourself today— not in a defensive manner, but allow your words to matter, by expressing them to those you normally wouldn't. Find your voice by imparting your wisdom to a struggling friend. Contribute at your work staff meeting. Your ideas are valuable. Break through the noise and boldly say, I am here! Your unique perspective matters and is valuable.

# 15

## Say Yes to Your Body

Take your hands and lovingly caress each part of your body that you may sometimes wish was different. Instead of focusing on what you may think is wrong with your physique, say yes by complimenting your body out loud. Give thanks for your strong, beautiful, capable, and unique vessel.

OCTOBER

# 16

~

## Say Yes to Conflict

Oftentimes, you may perceive conflict as a negative interaction that will dredge up antagonism, causing you to feel uneasy, upset, or inferior. Say yes to conflict by recognizing it as an opportunity to stand up for yourself, express yourself, and maintain boundaries. Use your quiet strength today as you interact with others. Neither chase after nor avoid conflict, and be open to the ways in which facing conflict can be an act of self-care that propels you forward.

OCTOBER

# 17

~

**Self-care is giving the world the best of you instead of what's left of you.**

—KATIE REED

# 18

## Say Yes to Tiny Miracles

Choose to notice the little joys in the day—the cool wind blowing through your hair, the warmth of the grass under your feet, or the light emanating from a child's smile. Search for what uplifts you in even the smallest of ways. Acknowledge those things. See how many of these incredible miracles you can give your attention to and how the experiences make you feel cared for.

Finish these statements as you observe the world today:

*I notice . . .*
*I enjoy hearing . . .*
*I enjoy moving my body like . . .*
*I enjoy knowing . . .*
*I enjoy being with . . .*
*I'm so glad I can . . .*
*I'm grateful for . . .*
*I'm looking forward to . . .*

What you look for grows in your life. Plant the seeds of grateful awareness and watch joy grow!

**Breathe. Let go. And remind yourself that this very moment is the only one you know you have for sure.**

—OPRAH WINFREY

## New Flavors

Create a meal from scratch with a new and complicated recipe that you would never have tried before. Say yes to giving it a try! Expose your senses to new experiences with unfamiliar spices, fresh flavors, and unexplored textures.

# 21

## Say Yes to Failure

Today, take a big risk and be willing to fail. When you have already accepted failure as a possibility, you're free to try the impossible. Remember that it's okay if things don't turn out how you hoped. You are building courage and learning valuable lessons through your "yes" efforts by erasing "what-ifs."

Ask your crush on a date, request a raise from your boss, apply for that job that's a little out of your reach, or consider launching that business you've dreamed about. You can do it. Failure is just a part of the journey to success.

# 22

## Say Yes to You

Name aloud everyone for whom you feel responsible for caring. Be sure to name yourself, as well! You are the most important person that you care for. Remind yourself that it is an honor to have the highest responsibility of caring for yourself. As you move through the month, say yes to the role of caretaker, keeping yourself at the forefront as you care for others you love.

OCTOBER

# 23

~~

## Say Yes to Compliments

Write down all the loving words and compliments that you can think of that people have told you about yourself. Accept them as the reality about who you are. Say yes to compliments. What they observe in you is valid. Behold yourself anew through their eyes.

OCTOBER

# 24

~~

*I am creating a life in which everything that needs to get done will get done, and I will still have the time to say yes to the things that I love.*

# 25

## See the World Through New Eyes

Look at yourself with new eyes today. You damage yourself when you are not willing to be honest about who you are—from what makes you wonderful to what you need to work on. Write a list of your shortcomings. Read them aloud, then say to yourself:

*I accept me.*
*I am perfectly imperfect.*
*My flaws create the beautiful tapestry of my being.*
*As I grow and change, I am becoming more of who I am meant to be.*
*I say yes to me.*

## Give Yourself a Wink

Start your day by smiling at yourself. Look at yourself in the mirror and award the reflection with the biggest smile you can. Before you turn away, give yourself a motivating wink. Are you flirting? Why not? Know that today is an opportunity for you to say yes to the beauty in the day and yes to the beauty in yourself.

*I am not timing myself. It doesn't matter how slowly I move. I am proud of my progress. My speed is enough. I am exactly where I need to be. I say yes to my pace.*

# 28

## Say Yes to Asking for Help

Ask three people for help today. Don't just accept it. Seek it. When you don't reach out for help, especially when you need it the most, what message are you sending to yourself about what you deserve or how much you can take on? Learning to say yes to offers of kindness or love is self-care. Accepting help is a loving act of vulnerability. Today, ask and accept any help that is offered to you without reservation and with considerable gratitude.

    Did you know that when people help you, they feel a bond with you? Increase your connection with the people in your life by experiencing the sensation of being cared for—a double win because you help both of you at the same time.

OCTOBER

# 29

## When I open my heart, my mind is free.

—ANI TRIME

# 30

~

## Say Yes to True Stories

Stress is not what keeps you from caring for yourself. It's how you respond to stress and how deeply you accept the false story of stress. Every day you have a choice. You are not stuck. You are free to care for yourself amid your every-day life. You can say yes to yourself by choosing to respond in a life-giving way to everyday stressors. Create a life-giving story—in which you are the star—about a situation that makes you feel stressed.

OCTOBER

# 31

~

**And every day, the world will drag you by the hand, yelling, "This is important! And this is import-ant!" . . . And each day, it's up to you to yank your hand back, put it on your heart, and say, "No. This is what's important."**

—IAIN THOMAS

# Gratitude

**"Thank you" is the best prayer that anyone can say. Thank you expresses extreme gratitude, humility, and understanding.**

—ALICE WALKER

There's no way around it. Grateful people are happy people. It really does matter whether you see the glass as half empty or half full. It's not just semantics. What you tell yourself about your world informs your entire experience of it. When you choose to see the good and give thanks for it, your life transforms. That goes for every single area of your life—your relationships, career, family, friends, and opportunities.

Weave gratitude into your life this month, and invoke an extraordinary side effect of increasing optimism, sleeping deeper, reducing pain, boosting the immune system, bolstering confidence, and decreasing anxiety and depression. This November, don't let anything traverse your senses without expressing gratitude for it.

# 1

*Gratitude is a sacred space in which you acknowledge the good things that are purposefully always at work and present in your life.*

# 2

## Notice the Thankless

It is standard to say thank you for acts of service. Today, say thank you to someone for an act, big or small, that usually goes unnoticed. Look beyond the personal interactions you have that might require a thank-you—go out of your way to tell someone they're doing a good job, are helpful, make you feel safe, or inspire you. Caring for others, in turn, is caring for yourself.

## 3

# Witness the Morning

Watch the sunrise. As you witness the bursts of color staging a rebellion along the dark sky, give thanks for another day—another opportunity to walk out your purpose.

## 4

# Vision It

Make a collage of all the things for which you are grateful. You can find pictures in a magazine or on the Internet; even better, take them yourself. Take a picture of your bedroom, your children, a vase of flowers, whatever exists in your environment for which you are grateful. This is like a vision board, except these things *already* exist in your life.

Putting your gratitude into a visual form solidifies the reality of all there is to be thankful for. The more you visualize it, the easier it will be to notice more opportunities for gratefulness.

## 5

Life may not be the party we hoped for, but while we are here, we should dance.

—JEANNE C. STEIN

NOVEMBER

## 6

## Be Mindful

As you complete the mundane tasks of the day, talk to yourself, with gentle reminders of what you are doing: *I am washing the dishes. I am thankful for this moment.*

Instead of allowing your thoughts to drift off from the present, anchor yourself in the now. Be grateful for the gift of the moment, which is why it is called the present.

*I am grateful that my worth doesn't come from other people, whose opinions may be based on superficial things. My worth comes from within, and I know what really matters to me.*

## Give a Gift, Get a Gift

Choose someone for whom you are grateful in your life. Tell them three things that you appreciate about them or three reasons why you are grateful to have them in your life. Ask them to tell you the same in return. Write down their words, and read them when you need encouragement.

# 9

~~

Gratitude is an antidote to negative emotions, a neu-
tralizer of envy, hostility, worry, and irritation. It
is savoring; it is not taking things for granted; it is
present-oriented.

—SONJA LYUBOMIRSKY

# 10

## Rock Your Gratitude

Psychotherapists sometimes use transitional objects—items that symbolize something that is meaningful—to provide comfort when the actual comforting object is not available. Today, find a rock—any rock—to serve as your gratitude rock. Put it in your pocket or place it on your desk. Every time you see it or touch it, pause to think of one thing that you are grateful for in that moment. At the end of the day, touch the rock and pause to think of all the things for which you were thankful today.

# 11

*I am grateful for my ability to know when to pause. I give myself permission to take space whenever I am in need.*

# Birth Gratitude

Write a letter of gratitude for your birth. No matter your relationship with your mother, she gave you the gift of life. Write about why you are grateful for this gift. You can keep this letter for yourself as a celebration of your life. Or you can give the letter to your mother and share your gratitude. Either choice is an act of self-care.

**Let us be grateful to people who make us happy; they are the charming gardeners who make our souls blossom.**

—MARCEL PROUST

# 14

## Thank Your Vessel

As you move your body today, give thanks for your muscles, bones, and joints working together in unison to give you the gift of movement.

# 15

## Hear the Gratitude

Speak these truths out loud:

*I am grateful for the people in my life because . . .*
*I am grateful for my place of residence because . . .*
*I am grateful for my body because . . .*
*I am grateful for my mind because . . .*
*I am grateful for the mundane because . . .*
*I am grateful for all the unnecessary luxuries in my life because . . .*

## Why Gratitude?

Gratefulness is a beautiful, life-affirming practice on its own, but you can dive a little deeper and explore why you are grateful. When you have a why for your expression, it becomes embedded as a core value. Meditate on why you are grateful for the people, things, and experiences in your life.

## Who Loves You?

Write a journal entry about the people in your life who make you feel loved and supported. Name them one by one. As you write, tune in to how grateful you are to have those people in your life. What does it feel like to have the gift of their presence and involvement? What have they taught you about your-self and the world? What lessons have proven invaluable? Resolve to invest more in those relationships.

## Meal Pause

Pause before every meal to give thanks for the sustenance the meal is providing to your body. Giving thanks for the simple things creates an attitude of gratitude, allowing you to recognize abundance everywhere.

## 19

## Getting Your Gifts Back

Imagine for an uncomfortable minute that you have lost everything that you own and hold dear to you: your family, your home, your health, your intellect, and your career. These are grievous thoughts, and it's okay to sit with them for a minute. Now, take a minute to visualize each being returned to you, one by one. Open the gifts slowly, allowing yourself to experience the overwhelming rush of relief and thankfulness. Look at what beautiful gifts you have. Give thanks!

*I lack nothing. I have everything I need. For that I am grateful.*

# Gratitude Flip

When things go wrong, as they sometimes will, you rarely feel an immediate sense of gratefulness, but rather anger or bitterness at the unfairness of life. Sit with this feeling today, then choose to reframe it into gratefulness. Be grateful that the thorns in your life have roses.

Example: My tire went flat, and I had to sit on the side of the road and wait for a tow truck. Now I'm late for work.

Grateful flip: I'm so lucky I didn't hit someone or have an accident. I'm grateful that I have a job. I am thankful there is a service that will help me take care of this issue.

NOVEMBER

# 22

~

## Gratitude turns what we have into enough.

—AESOP

NOVEMBER

# 23

~

*My grateful heart attracts wonderful experiences and people into my life. I notice the good, and good comes to me. I am a magnet for all that is good, because I am grateful for the magnificence of this present moment.*

# 24

## What Isn't?

What's the opposite of being grateful for everything that is? Being grateful for everything that isn't. Express gratefulness for all your fears about things that never happened—all the evasions of danger, punishment, and deserved consequence. Feel thankful for the protection and guidance you've received in your life.

# 25

## All the Seconds

Today, you received the gift of 86,400 seconds. You spent 2 seconds reading the last sentence. Spend the next 2 seconds feeling gratitude for the remaining 86,396 seconds of the day.

Time is the only real commodity—the only truly irreplaceable currency. Invest it wisely and be grateful for its fleeting beauty.

# 26

## Pocket-Size Wins

*I am thankful for all the little operations that work behind the scenes in my life to support me. I am thankful for opportunities, the luck I create, and the grace I am given. I am thankful for the pocket-size wins and the baby steps.*

# 27

## Anticipate Your Needs

Anticipating bumps in the road is significantly different from worrying. Learning to anticipate problems before they arise takes care of your future self by reducing stress points and smoothing out your daily ride. Check to make sure you are leaving yourself enough time to get to work. Preplan snacks so that you always have access to nutrition. Pack a change of clothes just in case and feel thankful for your ability to care for your future self.

## 28

Give yourself the same care and attention you give to others and watch yourself bloom.

—HOLLY A. BAY

## 29

# Naked Thankfulness

Sleep naked tonight. Whether you do this always—or never have done this before—practice being at one with your body for your nightly rest. As your bare skin is caressed by the sheets, give thanks for the intricate beauty of your senses. Give thanks for nerve endings that travel throughout your body and up your spine to create sensual experiences in your brain.

NOVEMBER

# 30

~

*No matter what form this minute, hour, day, or month takes, I will find the goodness and squeeze it out, and for that I am grateful.*

# Rest

**You rest now. Rest for longer than you are used to resting. Make a stillness around you a field of peace. Your best work, the best time of your life will grow out of this peace.**

—PETER HELLER

Your life has inched forward one year, journeying an almost complete circumnavigation of the sun. This year might have brought moments of joy and moments of sorrow. Throughout the crests and valleys, you have cared for yourself deeply.

Now, rest. Rest in the knowledge of all that you have done and all that you are doing to take care of yourself. There is a season for productivity, a time for learning, stretching, growing, and breaking down muscles. Your muscles of intention are fortified through rest. Take this month to breathe, reflect, pause, and give space to all that needs to expand. Welcome to your month of rest.

# 1

~~

## Your Way Is Okay

Everyone rests differently. Your brain is wired in such a way that what may feel like rest for you may feel stressful for another. Embrace your own restful lane. Get to know yourself well enough to ascertain whether certain activities replenish you or not. You can explore practices such as restorative yoga, meditation, painting—whatever strikes you as restful. Make a list of the activities that feel restful to you and practice them one by one.

## 2

# Next Year's Letter

Give yourself a little gift by writing a letter to yourself, with the directive to read it a year from now. This should be a letter of encouragement. Remind your future self of who you are now. Explain how you intend to show up in the world next year. State that you admire yourself and why. Be vulnerable about the struggles you are currently overcoming. Tell yourself exactly what you need to hear when you are questioning your abilities or competence. It's time for a pep talk! Have fun with it.

## 3

# Checking In

Lie down on your back, on a soft surface. Check in with every part of your body, asking how it feels and what it may need from you to feel cared for. Pay attention to signs that certain areas may need rest or care. Is something upsetting you? Are you storing the tension in your body somewhere?

# 4

*I deserve to breathe deeply. I deserve to pause. I deserve to conserve my precious energy. I am worthy of taking the time and space I need to move through this day, and the next day, and the many days that follow.*

# 5

## Conscious Rest

Aim to stay in bed an extra 20 minutes after you wake up—awake, but quiet and without distraction. Resist the urge to pick up a book, a pen, or your phone. Don't hit the snooze button or go back to sleep. Instead, take the day in, gathering your thoughts, sitting with yourself, imagining your day in the most hopeful of ways before it even begins.

DECEMBER

# 6

## Active Rest

Refrain from strenuous, intense exercise, and focus on moving and stretching your body in a restful manner. Move purposefully and with strength, but don't push past a comfortable pace. Don't worry, you will still maintain and even increase gains in your physical body from active rest.

DECEMBER

# 7

## Do You Really Need To?

A busy life is not necessarily a productive life. When the unnecessary is evaporated, what you are left with is what you really want and need to do. The list is so much smaller than the volume that was in the container to begin with. Be intentional about finding moments of rest, by asking yourself this prior to every activity and commitment: *Do I really need to . . . and why?*

DECEMBER

# 8

*I am intentional about pouring rest into my spirit. I choose to use my time today to pause, exercise, and be thankful. Because of this, I feel fresh, well rested, and energetic.*

DECEMBER

# 9

## Schedule Your Rest

Creating intentional space for rest allows you to respond to the world from a place of focus, peace, and calm, rather than to react out of a sense of frenzied pressure. Rest allows you to be an observer—a position from which you will easily be able to gather more information than if you had zoomed by amid your busyness. Is your rest purposefully built into your calendar? Schedule it now in whatever form feels best for you.

DECEMBER

# 10

~~~

## **Embrace Boredom**

Do you remember what it feels like to be bored? Not bored in the sense that
you are stimulated but not entertained—bored in the sense that you are com-
pletely unstimulated, uninterrupted, and unaffected by any external factors.
You are so bombarded by constant stimulation that boredom has become a
rare experience. Today, occupy a space that allows you to be bored. See what is
propelled by this vacuum. Creativity is the child of boredom.

DECEMBER

# 11

~~~

*A slingshot must be pulled back to create the power to spring forward. Rest is
pulling back.*

## 12

~

# The Power of Five

When you are in a frenzied state of busyness, there is a part of you that yearns to unplug from the world. When you feel this tug, take a five-minute break—a true rest for five whole minutes. No distractions, no activities, no indulgences. Five minutes of rest provides a powerful sense of grounding and rejuvenation. Close your eyes, breathe deeply, and get quiet. If your mind is primed for rest, you will immediately snatch up the opportunity and make good use of it.

## 13

~

# Ignore the Urgent

There is always something that must get done. Things like the dishes, the laundry, the bills, and the recycling are all urgent in their own way. But when you prioritize rest, you can ignore what seems urgent to make ample room for the necessary act of caring for yourself. Today, turn a blind eye to the mundane urgent thoughts that plague you and turn a caring eye to the needs of yourself.

# 14

~

## Hibernate

Create your very own escape cave, a sanctuary with all of your favorite sense-stimulating items—objects that light up your sense of taste, sight, touch, smell, or hearing. It may be just a small corner in your room. Add in textures, aromas, and visuals—all the things that make you say ahh and feel at ease. Find moments throughout the day to sit in your space and enjoy some rest.

# 15

~

*I have so much to give because I am a well-rested, full vessel, overflowing with strength to attend to and contain every pressing issue.*

# 16

## Eye Rest

Taking micro eye rests throughout the day is recommended by doctors to relieve overstrained eye muscles and increase overall health in your ocular functioning. This is an excellent yoga stretch for your eyes, known to improve eyesight and even reverse sight issues. Rub your palms together to create heat and cup them over your eyes. Look up and then down 10 times. Look left, then right 10 times. Move your eyes in circles in both directions, 10 times slowly, then diagonally in both directions, 10 times slowly.

# 17

## Good Enough

Strive for good enough. Perfection eliminates your ability to rest. You will never attain it; thus, you must constantly seek it. Good enough gives you space to rest. Trust that you give your best in every moment, with the knowledge that what defines your best may change in different circumstances.

## Steam Clean

Create a sauna-like atmosphere in your shower. Exposing your body and respiratory system to steam releases tension in your muscles and your mind. The heat releases toxins from your body and skin. As you breathe the steam vapor in and out, imagine your body filling up with light air, creating buoyancy and ease.

**There is virtue in work and there is virtue in rest. Use both and overlook neither.**

—ALAN COHEN

DECEMBER

## 20

~

# **Your Little Secret**

Plan a day off but keep it your own little secret. Maybe you officially take the day off, but instead of running errands or acting as a caretaker, you spend the whole day by yourself, doing the very things that you love and that give you joy without anyone else's input or permission. Take the day for yourself and choose not to feel guilty about gifting yourself this private, restoring time.

DECEMBER

## 21

~

*I have permission to rest. I do not have to do all of the things, nor should I. I deserve to be replenished.*

# 22

~

## Stretch It Out

Stretch in the most loving way you can for your body. Lie down flat on your back, on your bed or on a yoga mat. Take some deep breaths. Slowly tighten the muscles in your body, hold for 10 seconds, then release every muscle group starting with your face and moving down your body to your neck, shoulders, chest, arms, hands, diaphragm, buttocks, thighs, calves, and finishing with your feet. Take a cleansing breath. Resume the activities of your day feeling more limber and refreshed.

# 23

~

*I have nothing to prove. I make my own choices. I will move when I feel called to move. Until then, I will rest.*

## Avoid the Snooze

You may usually set your alarm with some flexibility in mind so that you can hit the snooze button. Hitting the snooze button may feel like you're giving yourself more rest, but you're actually creating a disrupted sleep experience. Set your alarm clock for when you really need to wake up and give yourself the gift of uninterrupted sleep. You will in fact feel more rested. And if you awaken at the same time every day, then your body will naturally train itself to the time and awaken more easily.

**Tension is who you think you should be. Relaxation is who you are.**

—CHINESE PROVERB

# 26

## Usher in the Light

Open the window coverings as soon as you wake up. Just five minutes of sunlight in the morning boosts your vitamin D levels and assists in balancing your cortisol levels, helping you maintain a healthy weight and overall feeling of well-being. Usher in the medicinal light!

# 27

## Infuse Calm

Chamomile, lavender, lemon, jasmine, rosemary, cinnamon, and peppermint teas are wonderful choices for a restful experience. Take a warm liquid break today. Include one or more of these calming, clarifying teas. Before each sip, take a deep breath, inviting the aroma and the steam into your body through your nose and your mouth, welcoming the calm.

## 28

The extent to which you rest and care for yourself is directly related to the meaning that your life has, the impact that you will make, and energy and enthusiasm that you will bring into every room.

—UNKNOWN

## 29

## Overload on Cute

Studies affirm that viewing cute and cuddly creatures, such as puppies and kittens, decreases stress, elevates mood, and makes you feel happy. It's practically impossible not to smile when you see a picture of a sweet little creature. Smiling multiplies happiness. Take a small break and indulge in cuteness.

DECEMBER

# 30

≈

Almost everything will work again if you unplug it for
a few minutes . . . including you.

—ANNE LAMOTT

DECEMBER

# 31

≈

## Reflect with a Plan

Revisit your gratitude jar. Read each entry out loud. Reflect on all that you
have to be grateful for. Ruminate on your growth this year. You have done an
excellent job of self-care through all the yeses and noes that you have lovingly
disciplined into your life.

Rest in the knowledge that you are growing and flourishing under your
diligent, nurturing, personal care. And you will continue.

List three ways that you will maintain your self-care through the New Year.

# Resources

## BOOKS

*Atomic Habits: An Easy and Proven Way to Build Good Habits and Break Bad Ones* by James Clear. Written by the leading expert of habit formation, this is an excellent reference for learning how to form good habits, break bad ones, and transform your life.

*The Five Love Languages: The Secret to Love That Lasts* by Dr. Gary Chapman. The author outlines five different styles that relationship partners use to express and experience love.

*The Four Agreements: A Practical Guide to Personal Freedom* by Don Miguel Ruiz. The author challenges you to examine the basis of your lens through which you see the world and the four agreements that you form early on in life. He advocates changing these belief systems to attain personal freedom.

*Get Over "I Got It": How to Stop Playing Superwoman, Get Support, and Remember That Having It All Doesn't Mean Doing It All Alone* by Elayne Fluker. The subtitle says it all. Written by the host of the Support Is Sexy podcast, Elayne Fluker helps busy women redefine what support means.

*The Gifts of Imperfection* by Brené Brown. Embark on a self-love journey with Brené Brown, one in which she teaches you, through an understanding of your own shame, how to love all parts of yourself.

*The Power of Habit: Why We Do What We Do in Life and Business* by Charles Duhigg. This book clearly explains how habits impact every aspect of your life and how lasting change can be created by targeting your habits.

*Sacred Rest: Recover Your Life, Renew Your Energy, Restore Your Sanity* by Saundra Dalton-Smith. The author is a physician whose workaholism led to burnout. She takes you on a journey of healing your need to be busy and learning to care for yourself through gaining an understanding of the seven types of rest.

*Year of Yes: How to Dance It Out, Stand in the Sun, and Be Your Own Person* by Shonda Rhimes. The author reveals how saying yes to everything for an entire year changed her life.

## PODCASTS

*The Dr. Zoe Show: Redefining Your Superwoman.* In this podcast, Dr. Zoe shares her wins, fails, and tips for helping women develop strength in difficult relationships, especially that sometimes difficult one with themselves.

*Inhabit the Art of Radical Self-Care.* Monica Ballard gives an honest exploration of the art of radical self-care, including the many challenges you face as women and how to transform them.

*Simple Self-Care.* Randi Kay of NaturallyRandiKay.com is dedicated to teaching you how to take good care through connecting with the natural rhythms of the seasons and your own inner wisdom.

*Support Is Sexy.* Podcast host, journalist, and author Elayne Fluker helps women change their concept of asking for help by viewing support as sexy!

# Acknowledgments

To my five children, in the order of your appearance into this world, Sarah, Sacaiah, Sagian, Sullivan, and Sigourney: You have each taught me the most valuable lessons of my life. I thank you for the honor of shepherding you onto this earth and for the joy of being a part of your journey on this planet. I love you now and forever with every breath I have. I pray that you accept the gift that only you can give—the gift of self-care.

To my best friend and constant cheerleader, my sister, Yolanda: Your belief in me makes me think I can do great things.

To my first love, my mom: You gave me life, taught me to love psychology, instilled in me the value of my self-talk, read my first "books," and told me I could conquer the world.

To my "other sister" and best friend, Rosie: You would single-handedly beat up a mob for me—you never have, but I believe you every time you offer. Thank you!

To my friend first and assistant second, Cristine: Thank you for taking care of the details so that I could do what I love.

To my dad: I miss you—you left too soon.

And to my husband of 26 years and counting, Stan: Thank you for putting up with me, all the late nights, and the whirlwind of serendipity that comes with loving me—I love you.

May you all care for yourselves well!

# About the Author

**Dr. Zoe Shaw** is a licensed psychotherapist, motivational speaker, podcast host, life coach, and fitness fanatic. She is a wife and mom of five. She is passionate about helping women develop strength in difficult relationships, including that sometimes difficult relationship with themselves.

After 15 years in traditional psychotherapy practice, Dr. Zoe jumped off the couch and now helps clients using a different modality with a mix of virtual therapy, coaching services, and programs designed specifically for women trying to have it all, who sometimes struggle in the superwoman game.

Dr. Zoe is the author of the Ask Dr. Zoe column for the Grit and Grace Project's online women's magazine, and she has been featured on OprahMag.com and in *Recovery Today* magazine. She writes about helping women redefine their strength. Find her on Instagram and most social media: @DrZoeShaw. She lives in Southern California with her husband, their kids, and a gang of labradoodles.